THE GERMANS IN AUST[E]

Germans came on the First Fleet, and ~~by 1900 they~~ were the fourth-largest European ethnic group on the continent, behind the English, Irish and Scots. Most settled on the land, and place names like Hahndorf, Hermannsburg and Fassifern speak eloquently of their presence. Others excelled as explorers, scientists, artists and entrepreneurs – and the names Leichhardt, von Mueller, Strehlow, von Guérard and Resch's Brewery feature prominently in Australian history and culture.

Two world wars soured relations between Australia and Germany, halted immigration, and shadowed the lives of many German-Australians. But the wounds healed surprisingly quickly, and the postwar migrant ships brought a second wave of German speakers. These 'invisible' immigrants proved to be popular New Australians.

Today there are some 700 000 Australians of German descent. Notable contributors to social, economic and cultural life range from Harry Seidler, Tim Fischer and Wolf Blass to cricketers Carl Rackemann and Darren Lehmann. The interest of German Australians in family background and ancestry is flourishing.

Jürgen Tampke holds a fellowship at the School of History, University of New South Wales. His books include *Czech–German Relations and the Politics of Central Europe* (2002).

THE GERMANS
IN AUSTRALIA

JÜRGEN TAMPKE

CAMBRIDGE
UNIVERSITY PRESS

CAMBRIDGE UNIVERSITY PRESS
Cambridge, New York, Melbourne, Madrid, Cape Town, Singapore, São Paulo

Cambridge University Press
477 Williamstown Road, Port Melbourne, VIC 3207, Australia

Published in the United States of America by Cambridge University Press, New York

www.cambridge.org
Information on this title: www.cambridge.org/9780521612432

© Jürgen Tampke 2006

First published 2006

Printed in China by Bookbuilders

A catalogue record for this publication is available from the British Library

National Library of Australia Cataloguing in Publication data
    Tampke, Jürgen.
    The Germans in Australia.
    Bibliography.
    Includes index.
    ISBN-13 978-0-52161-243-2 paperback
    1. Germans – Australia – History.   I. Title.
305.831094

ISBN-13 978-0-52161-243-2

To Amaya Jane, Oscar Jürgen and Tobias Peter,
who are all of German descent

CONTENTS

ILLUSTRATIONS

Note: 1 acre equals 0.4 hectare

ACKNOWLEDGEMENTS

For kind assistance and useful suggestions I am indebted to Richard Cashman, Chris Cunneen, Richard Dreyfus, Rod Home, John Jennings, Lee Kersten, Hans-Jochen Kretzer, Bernd Marx, Alison Paech-Ujejski, John Perkins, Arnold Velden and David Walker. Kathleen Weekeley's and Jean Dunn's excellent editing advice greatly improved the manuscript. Rudi Karle's help with the technical side of the production is much appreciated. I regret that despite my best efforts I am unable to provide source details for some of the illustrations, and I would welcome any information from readers.

For a last time – thank you Colin Doxford. Having worked together for so many years on the topic of the Germans in Australia, he was still able – although already very ill – to lend a helping hand with the manuscript for this book. Sadly he was not able to see the final product. Finally, thanks to Christine for everything.

All shortcomings in this work are mine.

Jürgen Tampke
Todtnau, 2006

INTRODUCTION

Germans have played a significant part in the history of Australia. They were among the first Europeans to set eyes on the continent in the seventeenth and eighteenth centuries, and Germans began settling here – both as convicts and their guardians – from the first days of the colony of New South Wales. Arthur Phillip, the first colonial governor, was the son of a German–English marriage. His father, Jakob Alt, an English teacher in London, came from Frankfurt. His mother Elizabeth, née Breach, had arranged for her son to learn her husband's trade at the School of Navigation in Greenwich. Others of German background who set foot on Australian soil in January 1788 included Heinrich Alt, Sydney's first Surveyor General, and Phillip Schaeffer, Supervisor of the First Fleet. Alt played an important part in the design and construction of the new township, and Schaeffer became one of the earliest settlers in Parramatta and the founder of Australian viticulture.

In the nineteenth century Germans abounded among explorers, scientists, artists and entrepreneurs. Above all, Ludwig Leichhardt, a legend today, led the first European expedition through Australia's vast northwest, to perish without trace in a subsequent attempt to cross the continent from east to west. Ferdinand Jakob Heinrich Mueller (created Baron von Mueller by the King of Württemberg) explored large areas of the Australian Alps and the Snowy Mountains and was a member of A. C. Gregory's 1855–56 north–west expedition in search of Leichhardt. Between 1857 and 1873 he was Director of the Melbourne Botanic Gardens. There were three Germans in the ill-fated Burke and Wills expedition, and the expedition's artist, Ludwig Becker, was among its first victims. He and his Austrian friend, Eugene von

Guérard, left behind many magnificent paintings and sketches of life, landscapes and people of their time. Josef Herrgott explored the country around Lake Eyre, and Johannes Menge the mountain regions in the north of South Australia. The latter is known as the founding father of South Australian geology. Georg von Neumayer, founder of the highly productive Melbourne Flagstaff Observatory, was knighted by the Bavarian king.

Other prominent figures, to name but a few, include Wilhelm Blandowski, Government Zoologist of Victoria, Johann Krefft, Curator of the Australian Museum in Sydney, and Robert von Lendenfeld, an acclaimed zoologist and glaciologist. Last but certainly not least in this brief list is Amalia Dietrich. A woman scientist was a rare phenomenon in the nineteenth century, and Dietrich spent nine years in Australia assembling an enormous collection (Aboriginal artefacts, birds, reptiles, insects and plants) for the Hamburg-based shipping house J. W. Godeffroy.

In the cities and towns, German businessmen prospered. Johannes Detogardi set up the first photographic studios in Sydney, while Wilhelm Lindt was one of Melbourne's early photographers. Carl Vahland, Bendigo's chief architect, designed most of the town's magnificent buildings; Friederich Mencken did the same in Newcastle. Brothers Edmund, Emil and Richard Resch founded Resch's Brewery, and Charles Rasp, having detected large silver deposits around Broken Hill, was among the founding fathers of the Broken Hill Proprietary Company (BHP). Some struck it rich in the goldfields. Bernard Otto Holtermann discovered the largest specimen of reef gold at Hill End near Bathurst in October 1871. He invested his money wisely, built a magnificent house for his family at St Leonards, and then devoted most of his life to his real passion – photography. His pictures of the goldfields, the New South Wales countryside, and in particular his panoramic shots of Sydney, provide an excellent record of the colony at the time. In Queensland, Heinrich Paradies and Friedrich Pfeiffer discovered the Day-Dawn goldmine near Charters Towers, which netted them several million pounds sterling. Pfeiffer in particular used his fortune to contribute to the profitable development of the Burdekin region.

Most German immigrants before the Great War (approximately two-thirds of them) went to the countryside. A combination of religious and economic reasons account for the fact that South Australia was the first colony to receive a large number of German settlers in the late-1830s and 1840s. Klemzig, Hahndorf, Lobethal, Tanunda and smaller hamlets in the Barossa Valley trace their origins to these times. In the third quarter of the nineteenth century industrious agents on commission from the colonial governments of Victoria, New South Wales and Queensland brought in close to 30 000 German-speaking newcomers from various parts of central Europe – and the subsequent chain migration was to more than double this figure.

In Victoria, they went first into the hinterland of the rapidly expanding capital and later into the wheat belts of the Wimmera and Mallee districts. In New South Wales, the country around Albury and Holbrook ('Germantown' until 1914) and the Riverina became the most popular regions, but many German families settled in the Illawarra and Bega districts, the Hunter Valley, the Mudgee region and Grafton and its surroundings. In Queensland, immigration was mainly to the southeast: the Logan district south of Brisbane, Rosewood Scrub west of the capital, Fassifern, the Lockyer Valley, the Boonah district and the Darling Downs. Subsidised immigration also brought German migrants to Tasmania, where they settled in the districts of Fingal, Glenorchy, Selby, Kingsborough and in and around Hobart. And although there was no subsidised immigration of continental Europeans in Western Australia, Germans accounted for the largest non-English-speaking group from Europe at the turn of the twentieth century. All told, by the end of the nineteenth century Germans were the fourth-largest European ethnic group in Australia, behind the English, Irish and Scots.

The second major wave of German immigration occurred in the third quarter of the twentieth century, when the wounds left by two world wars healed more quickly than expected. Over 100 000 German-speaking people came to Australia – mainly in the 1950s and 1960s – to make a new home. Like their predecessors a century earlier, they readily integrated into their new society – indeed an expert on Australian immigration has referred to them as 'invisible' migrants[1] – and they were popular newcomers. Opinion surveys taken not long after the cessation of hostilities in 1945 already ranked Germans as the most desirable migrants, after the British.

Germans played a big part in the construction of a new Australia. They became part of the phenomenal development from a largely homogeneous and monocultural community with a reputation for racial intolerance – 90 per cent of the population was then of European, chiefly British and Irish, stock – into a relatively tolerant multicultural, multiethnic society.[2] By the turn of the twenty-first century, close to 150 000 citizens listed a German-speaking country as their place of birth, and in the 2001 Census over 700 000 claimed German ancestry, making them one of the largest ethnic groups in Australia.

There is considerable ambiguity about the term 'German'. Today it is a political term. It refers to a citizen from the Federal Republic of Germany – or from its predecessor, the German Reich, which was created by the Prussian Minister-President Otto von Bismarck in 1871 and came to an ignominious end in 1945. But this definition of the term 'German' is far too limited. For most of the nineteenth century it was an ethnic reference, with few political connotations. To call someone a German meant that he or she spoke one of the countless dialects of central Europe. Politically, until the beginning of the modern nation state in the twentieth century, people owed their allegiance to a dynastic house – to the Grand Duke of Hesse-Darmstadt, perhaps, or the King of Württemberg, or the Emperor of the Habsburg Empire, a multinational community with many ethnic groups in east-central and southeastern Europe.

Until well into the nineteenth century a German could be a person from Alsace, which was ruled by the King of France, or from Hanover, which belonged to England, or from Schleswig, which was part of Denmark. A German could also be a citizen of the free city of Bremen, or a peasant from Brandenburg in the heart of Prussia. By the turn of the century there were about 300 political entities in the German-speaking lands, though the Vienna peace treaties of 1814 that followed the defeat of Napoleonic France reduced this number to 39.

Thus, before the creation of the German Empire, German immigrants asked about their background on arrival in Australia would say that they came from Baden, for example, or from the Palatinate, or from Silesia. And in those early days, since many spoke only their regional or local dialect, they would have faced considerable difficulties in communicating with one other. The Australian authorities could hardly be expected to discern such subtle differences, and hence they were all referred to as 'Germans'.

The concept of nationalism was new in European history – the idea of a German, Polish or French nation did not enter European thinking until the nineteenth century and did not reach its full force until well into the twentieth. When Otto von Bismarck achieved unification of Germany, the Prussian King Wilhelm III was crowned German Kaiser Wilhelm I on 18 January 1871, and the spirit of *Deutschtum* (Germandom) was born, there were close to ten million Germans living outside the German Empire (not counting the German population of Switzerland). Austrians and the German-speaking parts of the Bohemian Lands (today's Czech Republic) remained with the Habsburg dynasty, and there were substantial German communities in towns along the Baltic coast and throughout southeastern Europe. An equally large number of non-Germans were living within the new Germany. Most of them were Poles in Prussia's eastern provinces; and the Sorbs or Wends, a small Slavonic community, had been living under Prussian rule for a long time. In the west Bismarck had annexed Alsace-Lorraine, which meant that many French people had fallen under German rule, as had a small number of Belgians. And there were Danes in the southern part of Schleswig. In this book then, the term 'German' is used in its ethnic sense, to mean all German-speaking people. It includes not only those who lived in the state created by Chancellor Bismarck, but all German communities throughout Europe.

The implications of Bismarck's political achievement were soon to be felt world-wide and greatly influenced the history of the twentieth century – including Australia's. But initially they were of little concern to those who had decided to leave their German homelands for more promising shores in the Antipodes. A few did leave for political reasons. After the failure of the 1848 Revolution most revolutionaries went to the United States, but a small number made their way to Australia. The harsh, lengthy Prussian military service would also have persuaded a number of young men to head for distant shores after their homeland was incorporated into Prussia. The great majority, however, had little interest in politics. They were escaping the twin problems of nineteenth-century Europe: the impact of industrialisation coupled with a huge increase in population.

The story of German emigration and settlement has received much attention in recent years. There are now comprehensive works on the history of German settlements in all states, and thorough studies of German communities in the various cities and towns. Detailed studies of rural German communities throughout Australia tell us a great deal about the motives for emigration, adaptation to the new environment, education, religion, social life and so on. Among other things, these works paint a much clearer picture of what really happened to the Germans during World War I. By making use of this large body of scholarship, I hope to bring the story up to date.

1
WHY DO PEOPLE MIGRATE?

The century following the end of the Napoleonic Wars in 1814 witnessed the emigration of about 55 million people from Europe. The great majority – over 90 per cent – went to the United States, and a substantial number settled in Canada, South America, Australia, New Zealand and parts of Africa. Among those who turned their backs on Europe were six million Germans. Again, more than 90 per cent went to North America, but several hundred thousand headed for South America, in particular Argentina, Brazil and Chile, and about 70 000 came to Australia. In its wake this massive migration brought equally massive economic, political and social change around the globe.

Why these people left their traditional homelands for an uncertain future far away, in countries they often knew little about, has attracted interest among sociologists, demographers, historians, political theorists and other social scientists. There is general agreement that the transition in Europe from a predominantly rural to an urban industrialised society involved unprecedented economic, social and political changes. Over-population, famine and poverty (or the threat thereof) enticed people to seek more promising shores: countries that offered land ownership, employment, relief from want, and religious and political freedom. This strand of explanation is referred to as the 'push-pull' model. The desire to flee from a life beset by seemingly insurmountable difficulties and an unpromising future is the 'push' factor, and the prospect of a better society that promises security and perhaps even affluence is the 'pull' factor.

The push-pull theory is, of course, not to be taken in too simplistic or straightforward a way. There are indeed instances when human

Barque Eberhardt, *one of the ships bringing German migrants to Australia in the nineteenth century*

misery and poverty in Europe led to escape across the Atlantic or to the Antipodes. The devastating famines that followed the failure of potato harvests in the mid-1840s, for example, brought about a mass exodus from the British Isles – in particular Ireland – and the Continent. But normally the process of emigration is a lengthy one: the development of a desire to leave one's homeland that culminates in the eventual decision to do so is not a speedy affair. And before the planned migration is actually carried out, which demands yet another step to be taken, years may pass.[1] Moreover, it was normally not the most impoverished section of a community that took the decision to emigrate. The majority of migrants came from the lower to middle strata of society, such as crafts and tradesmen, artisans, handymen, small or tenant farmers and some day labourers with smallholdings. Even assisted emigration, which accounts for the bulk of migration to Australia since the early nineteenth century, requires that the emigrants have a small amount of capital to pay travel costs to and living expenses at the port of departure. At times, socio-economic reasons are intertwined with political or, to a lesser degree, religious motivations. And there were always those who left their home country for the sheer sense of adventure. But all told, the push-pull model provides the most convincing explanation of most of the German emigration to Australia, in both the nineteenth and twentieth centuries.

The push factor

Economically, it is customary to divide nineteenth-century Germany between west and east. In those parts of Germany that lay to the west of the River Elbe, farmers and their families at the beginning of the century owned and worked their own land. They often participated in small-scale manufacturing of various kinds in the periods between harvesting and planting. It was in the west that the great bulk of industry was established from around the middle of the century, replacing agriculture as the chief employer and rendering obsolete a large section of the traditional handicraft system. In the east, most of which was politically part of Prussia, aristocratic landlords employed day-labourers to till their huge estates, and as urban settlements were few, there was little opportunity for outside work. Industrial development remained modest, which meant that when the rapid population rise reached East Elbia, many rural dwellers faced a life of idleness and poverty.

By the nineteenth century the southwestern parts of Germany had already reached high population density. Most people were freeholders running a small block of land by means of what was still essentially subsistence agriculture. The longstanding tradition of dividing the farm among all descendants had fragmented arable land to such a degree that most plots were not viable. Unable to live off their land, these peasants had turned to home-based industries such as weaving and straw plaiting, or the manufacture of wooden tools and clocks. Sometimes referred to as the proto-industrial stage of economic development, this was generally a successful enterprise. Families used handicraft methods to work raw materials into finished goods, taking considerable pride in producing high-quality goods that could be exported to other regions. Clocks, tools, linen cloth and cotton thread were exported to the cities of western Europe, across the Atlantic, to the Ottoman Empire and even to distant places in Asia.

This system was dynamic. In normal times it provided many families with a livelihood, and in good times there was a modest degree of prosperity. But there were risks: a sudden decline might be caused by competition from another region, by harvest failure or by something as banal as a change in fashion in distant markets. Such events could leave a region to stagnate, with a population too large for its resources facing economic disarray. Because if the peasant was suffering, the situation became precarious all around. Small business, artisans and craftsmen relied upon a surplus of agricultural production to exchange for their goods and services. The saying was that 'if the peasant has money, all the world has money'. Blacksmiths, carpenters, cobblers, masons and wheelwrights all did well when the farmers could afford repairs and innovations. But with the gradual arrival of the industrial revolution, real hardship was knocking at the door.

The same was true in the east. Although legislation had freed all peasants east of the Elbe from serfdom in 1807, a subsequent host of Prussian decrees and laws meant that over the next half century 70 per cent of them lost access to land that was theirs by right.[2] After the defeat of Napoleon a grateful Prussian government thanked its rural population, which had provided the bulk of its fighting force, by restricting grants of lands to those peasants who had enough land to support a pair of oxen. Smallholders and all those with tenure of less than two generations lost their land. Fifty more laws passed in Prussia between 1816 and 1850 resulted in the transfer of one million hectares of land from the peasants to the landlords, and peasants who retained their land owed heavy compensation payments to their landlords.[3] The results of these policies were predictable:

> As production for cash profit became the theme of East Elbian agriculture, the owner became more determined to hold his labour force to a minimum; meanwhile the population grew at a fast rate. There came to be more people than the economic structure would absorb; in this sense, despite the sparse distribution of people and the high productivity of much of the land, there was overpopulation. The owner often found that he could even dispense with contract tenant labor and the housing and services it required, because he could rely on the free labor force always available. He would hire at plowing and harvest times, and he was free of obligation at other times. Crops became more specialized, and employment more seasonal; that was more profitable if labor was plentiful and could be hired and dismissed at any time. For the agricultural labor force it was a period of decline, of proletarianization.[4]

All this was accompanied by the onslaught of industrialisation, which after a slow start had gathered momentum in Germany by the 1840s. Initially, governments had been careful about uncontrolled industrial development. The Prussian government in particular was reluctant to give the go-ahead for railroad construction, mainly because of the huge costs involved. There were also fears that rail-roads would threaten security in wartime, and a restrictive banking policy led to a shortage of investment funds. But the rise of large-scale industry in Central Europe could not be halted for long, and nor could the entrepreneurial spirit of the age. Techniques of mechanisation, introduced in textile mills and coal mines, spread to other branches of manufacture and influenced the entire economic life of most Ger-man states. Gradually, banks and private investors began to transfer their funds from government bonds and commercial ventures to man-ufacturing enterprises. Owners of iron mills and other industrialists, financiers and businessmen asked for an end to the custom-ridden eco-nomic map of Central Europe, where a variety of monetary systems, commercial regulations, excise taxes and state boundaries crippled all efforts to liberalise trade and commerce. Eventually Prussia took the lead.

The formation of the *Zollverein* or customs union removed all trade barriers between most German states,[5] and less than a decade later the burgeoning industrial centres had all been linked by rail. Leipzig and Dresden were connected in 1839, Leipzig and Magdeburg in 1840, Dresden with Prague in 1840. The chief commercial and industrial cities in the Rhineland also linked together: Frankfurt with Mainz and Mannheim with Heidelberg in 1840, Düsseldorf with Elberfeld and Cologne with Aachen in 1841. By 1846 the Prussian capital, Berlin, was linked by rail to key harbours in the North and Baltic seas and to central Germany's chief economic regions. Due to pressure of com-petition from the new factories, the traditional local manufacturers of metal goods and textiles suffered. Southwestern Germany was hit par-ticularly hard by the low tariff trends of the *Zollverein*. A surplus of artisans of all kinds grew steadily, particularly after 1840. Scores of weavers went bankrupt; carpenters, saddlers, masons and blacksmiths saw their incomes decline drastically.

Population growth was adding to the social problems. Improve-ments in farming methods, diet, sanitary conditions and medical know-how led to a sharp decline in child mortality, which was the main reason for the leap in population across Europe throughout the nineteenth century. There was also a rise in marriage rates. In the tra-ditional guild system, only master artisans with full citizenship rights could marry, which meant that younger sons and daughters in both country and town could be left out. This marriage pattern meant that many who wanted to marry were forced to wait. But with the flourish-ing trade in manufactured goods in the early decades of the nineteenth century, urban guilds often had to recruit workers from the country-side. Manufacturing work, combined with a small agricultural holding, could enable a young couple to marry and start a family. And because children could from an early age add to the family income, there was no obstacle to having as many as possible. Earlier and more numerous marriages had obvious demographic consequences.

Within the borders of the later German Empire the population rose from 20 million in 1820 to 35 million in 1850 (and increased by a further two-thirds in the next half-century). Governments in some of the western states tried to stem the tide by introducing marriage restrictions.[6] In the east, where the *Rittergutsherr* (the noble estate owner) reigned supreme, less subtle pressure was applied to counter population growth. In the duchies of Mecklenburg-Strehlitz and Mecklenburg-Schwerin, for example, marriage laws stipulated that no one without a home could marry and no one could get a home except from a landowner – and the latter, to keep the cost of his social responsibility as low as possible, was not eager to see the population on his estate rise. Thus in the Mecklenburg states in 1850 there was only one marriage for every 269 citizens. This led to a big rise in illegitimate births, and it also encouraged young workers to leave their home districts: often a marriage licence could be obtained on condition of emigration.[7] Mack Walker's classic account of German emigration sums up:

> The westerner was squeezed, the easterner was dispossessed, or born without social birthright. Put the contrast this way: overpopulation leading to depression and emigration in the West resulted from the incapacity of the land, however intensely people were able to cultivate it, to support a rapidly growing population, as long as agriculture was inadequately complemented by industry and commerce . . . In the East, contrariwise, the problem was rather that the rigid social constitution and corresponding distribution of power and land made a situation where the growing population was not absorbed by the still plentiful land, because an increased and stable, year-round labor force was not profitable to the landowners – situation in part reflected by, in part aggravated by, the facts of peasant liberation. The solution lay in social change and the redistribution of land.[8]

Conditions such as these gave rise to massive emigration from Germany in the second half of the nineteenth century. There had been previous waves. Harvest failures, and the hunger and widespread poverty that followed years of food requisitioning during the Napoleonic wars, led to the emigration of 20 000 people in 1816 and

Advertisement for the German–Australian Steamship Company (reproduced in O. J. Seiler, Australienfahrt: Linienschiffahrt der Hapag-Lloyd AG im Wandel der Zeiten, *Herford, E. S. Mittler & Son, 1988, p. 53)*

1817. Relative economic stability meant little emigration for the next two decades, but renewed poverty – and the fact that the social problems had become clearly visible – revived this figure to an annual average of 20 000 by the mid-1830s. But with record bankruptcies in small businesses, the housing sector and most crafts in the late 1840s, coupled with the consequences of the 1846 famine – the second severe famine in two years – the floodgates opened. In the next four decades, well over five million people left Germany to find new homes overseas. It was not until the economic boom years of the 1890s, when industrial growth filled the gap between population growth and employment opportunities, that emigration from the German Empire petered out.[9] Half a century was to pass before the catastrophe of two world wars rekindled the push factor again.

The pull factor

As surviving letters, diaries and other forms of family records from German emigrants show, there is little doubt that economic dissatisfaction, uncertainty and worry about the future were the chief motives for most people. But emigration on a large scale also needs a pull factor. Conditions in the country of destination had to be right: immigrants had not only to be needed, but also to be welcomed. After World War I, for example, in the 1920s and early 1930s, the push factor was ample in Germany which, devastated by war, was on the verge of economic ruin. But migrants from the former enemy country were not welcomed.

In the nineteenth century they had been welcomed and indeed much desired by the Australian colonies. From the beginning the convict system as the chief source of labour had its drawbacks. Forced labour was inefficient, economically wasteful and much resented by the resident workforce. Nor did it make for a stable social system. In New South Wales, the 1830s witnessed increasing pressure from influential members of the colonial establishment to end further intake of convicts (the convict system was stopped in 1840). But the burgeoning economy needed labour. The answer was assisted immigration, which brought Australia's largest influx of new settlers, a crucial factor in the peopling of the continent. From the first bounty schemes in the 1830s until their abandonment in 1982, close to 3.2 million immigrants came to Australia by some form of assisted passage.[10]

Records of assisted immigration of Germans go back to 1825, when the Australian Agricultural Company brought out a number of German shepherds on seven-year contracts. Brothers William and Edward Macarthur subsidised the immigration of German shepherds and wine-growers throughout the 1830s. Bounty schemes began in 1835 in New South Wales, when the first set of regulations allowed for assisted immigration of foreigners (people from outside the British Isles) provided they were viticulturalists or were able to manufacture wine or oil. Labour shortages in the mid-1840s led to a new set of bounty regulations in 1847, this time allowing for the immigration of German-speaking people regardless of their professional background. A person bringing in immigrants was offered £36 for a man and his wife, £18 for a child over fourteen and £9 for a younger child. On arrival, the newcomers were assigned to various employers for two years of indentured service on low wages. Thereafter they were free to go their own way, seeking further employment or purchasing land if they had the means. As shipping fees were between £12 and £15 per person, immigration agents and other entrepreneurs could make a neat profit if they kept costs low and arranged for speedy employment of the immigrants upon arrival. Wilhelm Kirchner, for example, appointed immigration agent by the colonial government in 1847, made good use of this bounty scheme. About half of the approximately 6000 Germans who landed in Sydney between 1848 and 1859 were bounty immigrants or received some other form of assisted passage. So did the thousand or so Germans who went to the Port Phillip District between 1849 and 1851.

The discovery of gold in Victoria in 1851 dramatically exacerbated the problem of labour shortages in New South Wales. Thus a further extension of bounty regulations in 1859 specified that naturalised foreigners would be given bounty tickets if they wished to nominate relatives who were 'mechanics of any description, domestic servants, and persons of the labouring class'.[11] Queensland, which had become a colony in 1859, needed not only labour but also people to populate its vast territory. Having dispossessed the Aboriginal people, they could make generous offers. Immigrants who paid their own and their family's passage were entitled to land purchases worth £18 for each adult, and a further £12 at the end of two years, provided that, if not a British subject, he or she would be naturalised. If the fare had been paid by an agent, the latter was entitled to the first land order and the immigrant(s) to the £12 land order only. Johann Heussler, an immigration agent and merchant in Brisbane, managed to bring in up to 6000 Germans under this scheme over the next ten years.

To persuade potential migrants to make the final decision, the new country had to look promising, offering a much better life than their homeland. All agents were good at drawing an attractive picture of Australia, but Wilhelm Kirchner excelled in presenting a land where milk and honey flowed. After being appointed immigration agent by the New South Wales colonial government he speedily produced a little booklet, *Australia and its Advantages for Migrants*, which was published in October 1848 by the Frankfurt publishing house H. L. Brunner. Kirchner not only presented a most favourable account of the colony but also drew attention to shortcomings of other places interested in attracting European migrants. As the United States was already clearly the most popular destination – the journey was short and many Germans were already there – he placed great emphasis on that country's faults. But other places were also criticised: Canada was too cold, Brazil too hot, there were too many 'dangerous blacks' in South Africa.

Other Australian colonies also compared poorly to New South Wales. The Swan River settlement in the west was ill placed for trade; South Australia suffered from climatic extremes. Tasmania would be ideal for Europeans – but there was the problem of convicts. New South Wales, on the other hand, offered political stability, gave full citizenship rights one year after arrival, there were no wild and dangerous animals and, above all, no poverty and good economic prospects for people willing to work.[12] The booklet did well both in terms of circulation and of attracting immigrants. A second edition was published two years later, with the addition of fourteen letters from satisfied German settlers.

But the biggest pull factor throughout most of the second half of the nineteenth century was the discovery of gold, first in Victoria and New South Wales, and later in other colonies. Gold-seekers poured into Australia from around the world. Between 1851 and 1860 the continent's population trebled, from 300 000 to 1.2 million. In Victoria, which had become the most populous colony, there was a five-fold increase in this decade, from 90 000 to 544 000. This meant that eventually Victoria could dispense with assisted immigration altogether. Germans were well represented among the diggers: over 6000 are estimated to have arrived at the Victorian goldfields alone by 1861.[13] Strangely, gold fever did not infect about 1300 miners from mining regions in Germany's Harz mountains who had settled in and around Burra in South Australia, where huge copper deposits had been found mid-century.

Imperial Mail Steamship Großer Kurfürst *in Sydney (Hapag Lloyd Archiv, Hamburg)*

The push factor petered out by the 1890s, when the economic malaise behind the mass emigration had been eased by Germany's phenomenal industrialisation – in fact the country had to import labour. And the pull factor had also come to an end by this time. Several years of severe economic depression led to large-scale unemployment in all eastern colonies and put a temporary halt to the need to bring in large numbers of people. Gold, too, had run its course in Victoria and New South Wales by the final decade of the century (though the gold rush continued on a smaller scale in Queensland and was about to start in Western Australia).

Religion and politics

Religious persecution had played a large part in European migration since the time of the Reformation: the flight of the Huguenots from France in the sixteenth century, the expulsion of all Protestants from

Bohemia after the Battle of the White Mountain in the Thirty Years War, and the much popularised journey of the Pilgrim Fathers to the shores of North America – not to mention frequent persecutions and expulsions of Jews. The history books are full of examples. However, religion did not play a major part in German emigration to Australia.

The one notable exception, the famous emigration of 'Old Lutherans' to South Australia, was caused by religious harassment on the part of the Prussian government. But doubts have lately been raised about the view that inability to conduct church services according to one's convictions was the sole reason for the first major wave of Germans to head for Australia. By the time the first ships arrived in the colony the issue was more or less settled; hence religious persecution would not have been the chief motive for those who followed in the 1840s. There was one more case where religious persecution did result in emigration to Australia. In 1882 ten sisters of the Ursuline order fled Germany and ended up in Armidale, New South Wales, where they not only took over teaching in the Catholic schools but also greatly enriched the cultural life of this burgeoning New England town.[14] A large religious group did arrive in 1941 when over 500 Templers, a German Pietist community who had settled during the previous century in Palestine, were brought to Australia from Palestine and interned here. But they had fallen victim to wartime precautionary measures and hence do not fall into the 'migration caused by religious dissent' category.

Nor would political persecution rank among the chief factors behind German emigration to Australia. The aftermath of the abortive revolution of 1848 saw thousands flee from trials that might have resulted in death or lengthy imprisonment. The great majority, about 4000, escaped to the United States, yet a few headed down-under. Most '48ers' came on the *Princess Louise* and disembarked in Adelaide in August 1849. A handful more arrived in other colonies, where they vigorously participated in the political, social and cultural life of the growing capitals. Their stories make fascinating reading, but their number was too small to be listed among the significant push factors.

It is likely, however, that in the nineteenth century economic and political dissatisfaction did at times go together. Reports from parts of Hesse, for example, state that heavy taxation was a constant source of political disturbance, and one could expect that for some Germans coming to Australia, depressed living conditions went hand in hand with political dissatisfaction. The fact that one of the German clubs in Adelaide, the Allgemeiner Deutscher Verein, had a number of influential members with social-democratic leanings, as did the Club Vorwärts

in Melbourne, may well indicate that Bismarck's repressive labour legislation played a part in their decision to leave Germany. With the
current boom in research into family history, it would not be at all
surprising if documentation along these lines emerges. But evidence
so far does not support claims that they came in search of economic
betterment and a life removed from political oppression. The people
who left Germany for Australia during the big emigration wave in
the second half of the nineteenth century were conservative and law
abiding subjects. And here they became conservative and law abiding
citizens. Politics was not a major factor in nineteenth-century German
emigration to Australia. This was to change in the twentieth century.

The twentieth century

There was little German emigration to Australia before World War I
and even less in the years after. Whereas a major new assisted immigration scheme brought people in, chiefly from England, Germans could
come again as migrants after 1925 but had to find their own means
of both passage and settlement here. Nazi Germany's policy of racial
discrimination rekindled large-scale immigration, with the arrival of
German and Austrian Jews between 1937 and the outbreak of World
War II. After the war, vast parts of Europe lay in ruin, tens of millions
had lost their homes, political chaos reigned. It was from this pool that
the Australian government recruited new immigrants.

This time the social hardship was not the product of transition to
an industrialised society or of cyclical down-turns. The disaster was
man made: the result of a conflagration that demanded the mustering
of global resources to stop a political system that can only be classified
as insane. The Germans in particular had to pay a harsh price for the
murderous policies of their Nazi masters (and their collaborators).
German cities were bombed, rural regions suffered intense ground
warfare, and 8 million people were expelled from the eastern areas
(Silesia, East Prussia and Pomerania), most of which had been ceded
to the new postwar Poland.

The fury of the victors knew little mercy. A further 3.5 million so-
called *Volksdeutsche* were expelled from their homes in east-central
and southeastern Europe, most of them (approximately 3 million
'Sudeten Germans') from Czechoslovakia. They now lived in hastily
constructed refugee camps, where they were joined by hundreds of
thousands of people fleeing from the advancing Red Army and/or the
threat of communism. Sadly, many had good reason to flee: Croatians,

Estonians, Latvians, Lithuanians and Ukrainians were well represented among the auxiliary troops who had supported the Third Reich's Operation Barbarossa (the invasion of the Soviet Union) and the Nazi crusade against the 'Bolshevik–Jewish world conspiracy'. More sadly still, a disproportionately high number of them participated in the implementation of the 'Final Solution'. A cursory glance at the photographs or portraits smiling from the walls of the 'Captive Nations' clubs that sprang up in Australian cities and towns in the 1950s and 1960s shows whence the political winds had been blowing.

On the Australian side, politics also played a part. It was hoped that large-scale immigration from Europe would both assist ambitious plans for industrial development and help maintain the White Australia policy. Germans no longer came for economic reasons after the big postwar wave stopped in the early 1970s, as living standards in West Germany were then drawing equal to, if not surpassing, those in Australia. When the last big 'push' wave from Germany occurred in the early 1980s, there was no pull factor operating from Australia.

This time it was global politics that drove Germans to leave their country: the war in Afghanistan, the resumption of the nuclear arms race and the escalation of the Cold War under President Reagan led to the fear that *Mitteleuropa* might become the centre of a nuclear confrontation. In 1982, in the largest peace demonstration in the history of the Federal Republic, 300 000 people marched against the stationing of US mid-range rockets on German soil. The Australian embassy is said to have been swamped with applications – although since preference was no longer being given to European migrants, only a small fraction actually ended up here.[15] Australia was clearly seen as a safer place in case of a nuclear war.

Adventurers and stay-at-homes

The status of the push-pull theory as the chief explanation for migration has been challenged at times. The German sociologist Folkert Lüthke, for example, points out that emigration does not always take place when the conventional push factors (such as famine, poverty or persecution) are ample and the pull factor is also strong. His argument is that whereas conventional explanations rely largely on external causal factors – that the decision to emigrate is a reaction to outside influences – preference should be given to internal causal factors, i.e. to the role of the psyche. In his view some people are essentially sedentary (he uses the psychological term 'ocnophiles') and some are willing to leave their home ('philobates'). According to Lüthke, only philobates are ready to leave everything familiar behind to try something new.[16] This approach begs the obvious question that if psychological factors are the determining reason for people to emigrate, why do migration statistics differ greatly from decade to decade, sometimes even from year to year?

The push-pull theory provides a satisfactory explanation for the great majority of German immigration to Australia. But while immigration on a major scale covered only four or at most five decades, German-speaking people arrived here virtually every year – and many, if not most, of these newcomers were adventurers, or philobates. Regardless of their means or the political circumstances surrounding them, they were keen to explore the globe's vast offerings: different people, different cultures, the fascinating varieties of fauna and flora. Australia has always had a great attraction for philobates. They came as natural and social scientists, as artists, professionals, merchants and tradesmen, and many came with nothing but a sense of adventure – and remained.

2

THE FIRST FIFTY YEARS

First settlers and convicts

A study of European settlement in Australia traditionally begins with the arrival of the First Fleet – which, as we have noted, included several prominent people of German origin. Throughout the eighteenth century a number of German states, above all the House of Hanover, maintained close relations with the United Kingdom. The marriage in 1658 of the Elector Ernest August of Hanover to Sophia of the Palatinate, grand-daughter of James I of England, secured for the House of Hanover the British succession in 1714, by virtue of the 1701 Act of Settlement in favour of Sophia. With the death of both Sophia and Queen Anne in 1714 Sophia's son, the Elector Georg Louis, ascended to the throne as George I. This event marked the beginning of a 123-year-long personal union between the United Kingdom and Hanover – a union characterised by close political, economic, military and cultural ties. In 1737, on the initiative of George II, the Hanoverian town of Göttingen received its university, which soon established itself as one of the leading centres of learning on the Continent. Throughout the period of the union there was a regular exchange of teachers and students between Göttingen and Cambridge and Oxford universities.

British connections to the Electorate of Hesse-Kassel go back to the Seven Years War, in which English and Hessian troops supported Prussia against France, Russia and Austria. And the Elector of Hesse provided 18 000 soldiers to fight for the British in the American War of Independence. This military alliance, too, was accompanied by economic and cultural links.

Hence it is not altogether surprising that Governor Arthur Phillip's father was a German teacher from Frankfurt. The father of Augustus Alt, the first Surveyor of Lands in New South Wales, was Hessian. Jost Heinrich was a prominent member of the Hessian Legation in London, where for reasons not altogether clear he was known as Baron Alt. Although there is no record that this title was ever officially conferred, his son was also generally addressed as Baron Alt. Augustus Heinrich was born in 1731, the third of seven children, and educated at Westminster School. In 1755 he was appointed ensign in the king's 8th Foot Regiment, which was sent to Hanover to support Prussia in the Seven Years War, after which he became Engineer of Roads in the Scottish highlands. In 1777 he joined the Royal Manchester Volunteers with the rank of lieutenant and participated in the siege of Gibraltar where, according to the British commander, 'he distinguished himself in the most gallant manner'. George III appointed him Surveyor of New South Wales in 1786, and he played an important part in the design and construction of Sydney during the colony's first ten years. He married a convict woman, Mary Anne George, with whom he had two children. Having retired from service in 1797 because of failing eyesight, he was granted 330 acres in what is now the suburb of Ashfield, where the family is said to have run a small farm until his death in 1815.[1]

Phillip Schaeffer had served as a second lieutenant in one of the Hessian regiments fighting with the British during the American War of Independence. According to the records he was not very well suited to the office of superintendent and resigned after two years. Schaeffer then became one of the earliest free settlers, and planted Australia's first vineyard in the gardens of the newly built Government House at Parramatta in 1791. He is said to have been a prolific wine-grower, but to have squandered his fortune, being a keen drinker himself. He married Margaret McKinnon, transported because she had burned down her neighbour's house (allegedly through sheer jealousy). Alcohol eventually ruined Schaeffer's life and he died in the colony's poorhouse.

By the 1820s a number of German merchants had settled in Sydney.[2] The titled von Bibra family, a Franconian baronage with a family tree going back to the sixteenth century, had taken up residence in Tasmania. Francis Ludwig von Bibra published the first book aimed at enticing people to emigrate to Australia. *Description of the island Van Diemensland a most remarkable colony in the South Seas: A handbook for those who want to emigrate* was published in Hamburg in 1823. His son Benedict moved with his family in the 1830s to Western

Australia, where he tried unsuccessfully to introduce a bounty scheme for immigrants from German-speaking countries. Four of the six sons of Baron Heinrich von Stieglitz, originally from Pilsen in Bohemia, played an active part in the early settlement of Tasmania, while the remaining two brothers were among the first settlers at Port Phillip.[3]

There were not many people of German origin among the convicts who made up the bulk of both the population and the workforce in the first decades of the colony. Reference has been found to seven Germans deported between 1792 and 1829, six to New South Wales and the seventh to Van Diemen's Land and, to judge by their names, a handful of Germans ended up among the convicts in Western Australia.[4] Statistically, their number is too insignificant to dent the conventional account that the convicts came from England, Scotland and Ireland. But German prisoners nearly arrived in larger numbers. In January 1835 the consul-general in London for the Hanseatic city of Hamburg, J. C. Colqhoun, contacted the office of the Australian Agricultural Company (a London-based enterprise that held rights over a million acres in New South Wales) about a letter he had received from Senator Hudtwalcker, the chief of Hamburg's police. Hudtwalcker referred to the crowded state of prisons in his city and to repeated endeavours to get rid of some of the inmates by transportation to remote countries. He enquired whether the Australian Agricultural Company would be interested in the acquisition of reliable and cheap labour. The letter illustrates the social consequences of the decline in the traditional guild and handicraft system: a sharp rise in criminality brought about by large-scale unemployment. In Hamburg the prison problem was aggravated by the high rate of recidivism. As Hudtwalcker put it, 'from the smallness of our territory, any petty offender is always forced back again into the scene of life from which he emerged; whereas in the larger states their removal into distant places of abode takes them from their first excuse for their return to former practises'.[5]

Both the chief of police and Colqhoun were at pains to emphasise that the convicts selected would be chosen from the youngest and healthiest of both sexes. To make the proposal even more attractive, only prisoners convicted of minor crimes were to be sent to New South Wales, prisoners who, 'having deserved punishment for their crimes, are still more the object of pity, than of the severity of the law'. In fact, the Australian Agricultural Company was getting a real bargain: 'our convicts are not so dangerous as the English and I believe you may safely rely upon them never entering into any combination to withdraw themselves from the laws of the colony they are sent to'.[6] For

the convicts, transportation was an ideal way to redeem themselves –
a mild punishment that was bound to bring success.

Surprisingly, in the light of such a generous offer, the first reaction
of the Australian Agricultural Company was unenthusiastic. On receiving the request from Hamburg, the company's management committee
recommended to the Court of Directors that 'they would not be justified in entertaining at the present the proposal made to the company'.[7]
On second thoughts, however, it occurred to the directors that the
600 000 acres granted to the company on the Peel River and the
Liverpool Plains, in exchange for its Port Stephens grant, had to be
adequately staffed, and that increased demand for convict labour was
making it difficult to find. So the final news was good for the city of
Hamburg – the company agreed to take a large number of prisoners,
if they could be supplied.

Protracted negotiations about shipping costs, the convicts' sex (the
company wanted male labourers only), terms of work and the spiritual guidance of the prisoners continued over eighteen months.[8] At
last a first transport of 40 convicts was ready to leave Hamburg harbour, when the news arrived that the Secretary of State, Lord Glenelg,
had reversed his earlier stance and called the whole scheme off. The
colonial establishment in New South Wales had got wind of the venture and, keen to end the convict system altogether, strongly protested
against a further increase in prisoner intake – and foreign convicts at
that. Edward Macarthur, eldest son of the influential John Macarthur,
succinctly put their case:

> Upon a recent occasion I learned that there was some projects
> importing to the Colony a number of Convicts from the State of
> Hamburg. I remonstrated against so unnecessary appropriation of
> foreign Crime, foreseeing that it would be injurious to the Character
> of the Colony; and the System, once commenced, might lead to New
> South Wales becoming a general receptacle for Criminals from every
> part of Europe.[9]

Importing free labour from the Continent proved equally difficult during the colony's first half-century. The Australian Agricultural
Company managed in 1825 to employ four shepherds, Carl Rantsch,
Gottfried Hadel, Friedrich Lehmann and Johann Christian Pabst, on a
7-year contract. Little is known about the enterprise, and of the shepherds' fate we know only that Pabst did well for himself. On completion
of his contract he became the 'postilion' for the run between Tarcutta
Creek and Billibung. He married a free settler from Dublin and

established a prosperous homestead at Billibung. Friedrich Bracker arrived in 1829 with 200 Merino sheep, selected by him from Prince Esterhazy's flock in Silesia, and a great deal of expert knowledge in sheep breeding. In 1830 William Macarthur, of the prominent pastoral family, employed a German wool-classer, known as Herr Klotz, to manage his sheep and wool business.

As bounty regulations allowed immigrants from the Continent to qualify for the scheme in exceptional circumstances only, no significant group of Germans arrived until 1838, when Edward Macarthur managed to sign up six wine-growers from Hesse's Rheingau region and their families.[10] As they proved industrious workers, the Macarthurs intended to contract further groups from the same region three years later. When the colonial government in London withdrew the clause that permitted larger numbers of non-British wine-growers to work in the colony, William Macarthur wrote an angry response:

> It may naturally be asked how it happens if soil and climate be so favourable for vineyard culture that we not see our hills clothed with vines and their produce the common beverage of every class in the community. The reply is simple and obvious, it is owing to the almost entire absence of practical acquaintance with its details. Had our Home Government fulfilled its duty there would have been conveyed to our shores during the prevalence of the Bounty System of Emigration two or three hundred German, Swiss or French vine dressers. Had this been done vineyards ere this would have become common amongst us. Not only have they omitted to perform that which would have been the act of a wise and paternal Government but they absolutely interfered with private arrangements . . .[11]

So it was up to the new colony of South Australia to take a more liberal approach to non-British immigration.

The 'Old Lutherans'

The beginning of large-scale German immigration into Australia is marked by the arrival in Adelaide between November 1838 and January 1839 of fours ships from Hamburg carrying almost 500 Prussian 'Old Lutherans'. The background to this enterprise is in many ways surprising, because the immigrants had left their homeland largely because of religious persecution. This in itself was an astonishing affair, as the Kingdom of Prussia had always prided itself on its record of religious toleration. In particular, the emigration of 20 000 Protestants from the

Salzburg region of Austria to Prussian Lithuania in the early 1730s has been viewed as evidence of the Prussian state's enviable record on the issue of religious freedom. The bizarre picture of policemen and soldiers breaking into churches, harassing and arresting harmless worshippers and gaoling so-called ring-leaders had its origins in the decision of the Prussian king, Frederick Wilhelm III, to unite the two Protestant religions – the Lutherans and the Calvinist 'Reformed' – into one 'evangelical Christian' community. To achieve this, the new United Church was to become the life ambition of a monarch who is otherwise ranked as one of the duller and less colourful Prussian rulers.

A division between the Calvinist religion of the Prussian ruling house of Hohenzollern and the Lutheranism of the overwhelming majority of its subjects dated back two hundred years, and the idea of a union had occupied the attention of rulers ever since. Only Frederick the Great was opposed to the notion, and his great nephew, Frederick Wilhelm III, who ruled from 1797 to 1840, had other ideas. In his resolve to bring about a union of the two faiths, Frederick Wilhelm was encouraged by the eighteenth-century emigration of Huguenots and Dutch settlers into Prussia, which had added substantially to the Calvinist population. He also believed that the doctrinal tenacity of Lutherans had been considerably weakened by the influence of pietism and rationalism over the course of the eighteenth century. In these assumptions he was basically correct. However, he under-estimated the determined opposition of a minority unwilling to compromise on Lutheran doctrine.

The process commenced symbolically on 31 October 1817, the tri-centenary of Luther's nailing of his 95 theses to the church door at Wittenberg, when all Lutheran and Calvinist churches undertook a joint communion. On the same day, the two Protestant congregations in the king's Garrison Church in Potsdam merged into the first congregation of the newly formed United Church. Frederick Wilhelm believed that this step would set an example that all congregations in his lands would follow, and his expectation proved correct. By 1825 more than two-thirds of the Protestant churches in Prussia had become members of the United Church, with its new liturgy and order of service. Encouraged by this apparent success, Frederick Wilhelm decided to use the tri-centenary of the Augsburg Confession on 4 April 1830 to consolidate the process of unification by a set of new measures, which effectively took the unification process a step further away from traditional Lutheranism.

To use this key date in the annals of Lutheranism as the symbolic occasion for further reforms was an ill-judged move, and the dissatisfaction that had been smouldering in parts of Prussia's eastern provinces reached bursting point. The centre of opposition was the theological faculty of the University of Breslau, where the Professor of Theology, Johann Gottfried Scheibel, was refused permission to use the traditional Lutheran Wittenberg liturgy. Scheibel was soon joined by a growing group of traditional 'Old Lutheran' pastors, who consequently were suspended or dismissed from office. The conflict reached a first climax on Christmas Eve 1834, when armed soldiers broke into the town church in Hönigern, and over fifty people were arrested and many injured.[12]

It was not surprising that most of the conflict occurred in Silesia. The province had been part of the (Catholic) Habsburg Empire until its forced incorporation into Prussia by Frederick II in 1740. Having been minorities in a largely Catholic land, the Lutheran communities in Silesia had developed a particularly strong and independent spirit. By the mid-1830s, opposition to the union had spread beyond Silesia to parishes in neighbouring Brandenburg, Posen and Saxony which, like the Silesians, insisted on being called Lutherans and rejected all practices of the United Church that did not adhere to traditional Lutheran doctrine. When this led to further repressive measures, a number of Old Lutherans decided to call upon another traditional right – to leave the country altogether.

The first congregation to announce its intention to emigrate from Prussia was that of Klemzig and surrounding villages in the Brandenburg district of Zillichau. The pastor here, August Christian Kavel, went to Hamburg in early 1836 to look for a place of emigration for his congregation. While investigating possibilities in North America or the Caucasian region of the Russian Empire he made the acquaintance of George Fife Angas, who told him about the new South Australian settlement scheme and suggested that Kavel and his flock move to that colony. Kavel, impressed by Angas's deep religious convictions and the promise of economic and other assistance, went to London, where the two men soon reached an agreement. In July 1836 Kavel proposed a detailed plan to his congregation at Klemzig. At the same time, and with the support of the British consulate in Berlin, he applied for permission to emigrate to Australia.

The news that almost 500 subjects were planning to leave the state because of religious persecution did not go down well with the Prussian authorities. A witch-hunt for 'ring-leaders' and 'fanatical preachers'

Pastor August Kavel (Mortlock Library, State Library of South Australia)

proceeded unabated, and the Prussian ministry of church, health and educational affairs managed to delay the permission to emigrate for almost two years. But in the end the king had to yield, and on 8 June 1838 the Zillichau Lutherans made their way by boat along the rivers Oder and Elbe to Hamburg harbour. The spectacular journey, marked by constant singing and praying, attracted the attention of thousands of onlookers all along the way. In Berlin, when passing the riverside restaurants where the capital's well-to-do were taking refreshments while listening to music, the pious Christians loudly sang the hymn 'Follow Me Says Jesus Our Hero'. The Prussian king is said to have lost his appetite:

Klemzic, a village of German settlers, *lithograph by George French Angas, 1846* (*State Library of South Australia, B 15276/12*)

> Don't like to hear about it; don't like it. Unbelievable in a country where there is freedom of religion and freedom of thought – But freedom does not mean anarchy, lack of restraint and refusal of obedience. Those disturbed people call themselves Lutherans. What would Luther say, were he still alive . . . Still, I wish them well.[13]

But other people viewed the event very differently. Senator Hudt-walcker also watched as the Old Lutherans approached Hamburg harbour:

> One fine evening as I was walking across the town embankment, I heard the melodious sound of many men's and women's singing hymns, coming from the harbour . . . As singing like this has not been heard for many years past, I became curious and had a boatman row me over there. I found four large Oder River barges filled to overflowing with men, women and children. This was the story I was told. These people, nearly 400 in all, all came from Klemzig near Zillichau and a few neighbouring villages. They were Lutherans and were forced to emigrate on account of their faith, to South Australia, a new British colony. What, I thought, Lutherans forced to emigrate from Prussia on account of their beliefs? Thereby must surely hang a tale! They must surely be bigots, of whom we hear so much, or

mystics and fanatics. I therefore inspected their ships and engaged them in a conversation. The vessels were meticulously clean and neat, although they were almost overloaded, and the serene and friendly expressions on the people's faces were in keeping. From some of the men, who were pointed out to me as leaders, I heard the following account.

At first, because they did not understand the issues, they had allowed themselves to be persuaded to accept the union with the Reformed Church, but later had become convinced that the doctrine of this church concerning the Lord's Supper was not in accordance with the scriptures. They therefore repented their decision, and their preacher also refused to accept the new liturgy. He had finally been dismissed and had already been for the past two years in London . . . but now he is to go with them to South Australia and resume pastoral care for them there . . . Because they were unable to acknowledge a United Church preacher, they had, it is true, begun to baptise their children themselves, and to celebrate the communion together . . . The authorities then intervened and had forbidden them to do this, under pain of punishment. One woman told me that she was in prison four times . . . I made enquiries as to the conduct of these people on board their ships, 'Exemplary' I heard from all sides. No quarrelling, no swearing is to be heard on the barges. They conduct Devotions both morning and evening, with hymn-singing and prayer reading . . . I went back on shore, cordially wishing the poor Klemzig folk a safe journey and a new home in a land where they can worship God after their own fashion.[14]

From Hamburg onwards, things proceeded smoothly for the Lutherans. Their first stop was Plymouth, where they were joined by Pastor Kavel who, in order to avoid being arrested, had decided to arrange the emigration of his flock from England. After a relatively calm journey the *Bengalee* was the first of the four ships to berth at Adelaide on 16 November 1838. The others followed over the next two months. Although there would have been employment for everyone in an expanding Adelaide, the Klemzig Lutherans insisted on staying together and leased a plot of 144 acres about 8 kilometres north of Adelaide on the Torrens River. Here they built a small village, which they named in memory of their old home, Neu-Klemzig. The picturesque new settlement, built in the German tradition of a *Hufendorf* (farmlet village), drew many favourable comments from the English-speaking residents. A contemporary newspaper depicts the newcomers as assiduous 'as an English bee at spring time':

[The men] weed, water, fish, milk, wash and built wooden
houses'. . . [and the women were] just as industrious, busy baking
bread, making butter, cooking and many other things. There is no
one lazy soul. Even the School children who are still too young to
work, receive regular school lessons conducted by their never tiring,
outstanding pastor.[15]

Given the industriousness of the new settlers and the fertility of the
soil, the Germans were soon able to provide Adelaide with their produce. Klemzig became one of the town's main suppliers of vegetables,
fruit and dairy products. The *Zebra*, which had a particularly arduous
journey – the ship was struck by typhoid fever and scurvy – arrived at
Holdfast Bay on 28 December. The passengers were fortunate, however, that William Hampden Dutton, one of the three Dutton brothers
who were pastoral entrepreneurs in New South Wales and South
Australia, offered them the lease of 150 acres in the Adelaide Hills,
30 kilometres southeast of Adelaide. In gratitude to their captain, who
had given them so much assistance on the journey, they named their
new settlement after him, Hahndorf.[16] Frugal and industrious, the
Germans managed not only to pay back within a few years the loans
they had raised for the journey and for the purchase of land, but also
to pay for relatives, friends and neighbours to come to Australia.

By the time Pastor Gottlieb Daniel Fritzsche, who was to become
the second founding father of Lutheranism in Australia, arrived in
Adelaide on 28 October 1841 with his congregation from Posen, the
religious confrontation was more or less over. Bad international pub-
licity and the shady legality of the Prussian government's actions meant
that the heat had gone out of the conflict even before Frederick Wilhelm
III died in 1840. Some emigrants may have left their homeland for fear
of renewed persecution, but the chain migration that followed over
the next few years was largely driven by economic factors. To judge
by their social status – artisans, handymen, peasant smallholders and
landless labourers (the very occupations most affected by the social
malaise in their places of origin) – social and economic motives most
likely played a part from the very beginning. Many people would have
attached themselves to the Old Lutherans as a way out of difficult
circumstances.[17]

Most of the new arrivals, as well as some of the original German
settlers, began to move into the Barossa Valley, 60 kilometres north of
Adelaide, by 1842. Approximately 1200 Germans had settled in South

Australia by 1845, as chain migration was gathering momentum. The publication of a small booklet entitled *Reports of German Settlers in South-Australia* depicted a prosperous land of milk and honey. One of the letters stated that 'the country is so rich and fertile that everyday they eat the most beautiful cake . . . Moreover . . . they can afford tea and coffee daily for breakfast and dinner . . . and much fat meat is eaten, such as mutton and pork, which is good for our well being.'[18] Such comments would not have been lost on relatives, friends and former neighbours at a time when Germany was in the grip of a severe food shortage caused by the failure of the potato crop in the mid-1840s. The majority of nearly 9000 Germans living in South Australia by 1860 were from the Old Lutheran districts of Brandenburg, Posen and Silesia.

Economic prosperity was largely achieved, but religious unity remained illusory. At a meeting held at Bethany in the Barossa Valley on 16 August 1846, the Old Lutherans split into two groups. One, led by Pastor Kavel, became known as the United Evangelical Church in Australia (UELCA) or Immanuel Synod, the other, led by Pastor Fritzsche, called itself the Evangelical Church in Australia (ELCA). Differences had arisen over a number of theological questions, in particular the issue of Chiliasm (the belief in the imminent coming of the end of the world and the thousand-year empire of Christ). Whereas Kavel held millenarian views, Fritzsche rejected them as a misguided product of 'anabaptical zealotism' – irreconcilable with scripture. Further difficulties arose over the question of church organisation. Kavel favoured an independent church organisation based on the model of the era of the Apostles. Fritzsche accepted the need for a hierarchy and envisaged the creation of a world-wide centrally controlled Lutheran church. Whereas the UELCA continued to work and co-operate with Old Lutheran congregations in Germany, the ELCA was to establish close links with the Missouri Synod in the United States. This division meant, among other things, that many country towns in South Australia had two Lutheran churches. In fact, as both groups spawned smaller breakaway synods, in Tanunda (which had become the centre of German settlement in South Australia), there were eventually four churches, all bitterly opposed to each other.[19] It took more than a hundred years to heal the divisions.

3

SCIENTISTS AND
EXPLORERS

Australia gradually entered the European field of vision due to improvements in ship-building and navigation techniques, accompanied by steady advances in scientific know-how (sometimes referred to as the Scientific Revolution), the widespread spirit of inquisitiveness that accompanied the Age of Enlightenment and, last but not least, an insatiable thirst for economic gain. The German Hanseatic cities – Bremen, Hamburg, Lübeck or Danzig – were too small to establish an overseas empire but, because of the close links of some of the German states to the Netherlands and England, a number of Germans participated in the first European journeys to the Southern Hemisphere. Yde Hollemann from the north German Duchy of Oldenburg was second-in-command of the *Heemskirk* on Abel Janszoon Tasman's second voyage in 1644, and Ferdinand Lucas Bauer was the botanical artist during Matthew Flinders's circumnavigation of Australia in 1801.

Bauer, born in 1760, was the son of the court painter in the tiny principality of Liechtenstein. He grew up in Austria and in his early twenties was employed as botanical artist at Vienna University, where he met John Sibthorp, Sheridan Professor of Botany at the University of Oxford, who persuaded him to come to England. Bauer soon became widely known as a talented artist and, on the advice of Sir Joseph Banks, President of the Royal Society and unofficial director of the Royal Botanic Gardens at Kew, was invited to join a team of scientists and artists accompanying Matthew Flinders on his voyage in the *Investigator* to chart the Australian coastline. Bauer gladly accepted the offer. During the journey the civilian party went ashore at each landfall to explore the country and record their observations of the local wildlife. On completion of the expedition Bauer had made over 1000 drawings of plants and 200 of animals, of such fine quality that he is ranked among the world's greatest natural history painters. Fifty-two of his meticulous drawings are still on display at the Natural History Museum in London; the bulk of his remaining collection is today held at the Naturhistorisches Museum in Vienna.

But it was father Johann and son George Forster – who accompanied Captain James Cook on his second journey to the Pacific that lasted from 1772 to 1775 – who, above all, caught the interest of scholars writing about the early role of Germans in the history of Australia. Johann Reinhold Forster from the Danzig region of Prussia was one of the most eminent German natural scientists of his age. By the time he joined Cook he had already undertaken a major research project for the Russian empress, Catherine II, investigating the possibility of German migration into the lower regions of the Volga River. He is said to have been in command of a string of ancient and modern languages – seventeen altogether. The Board of Admiralty, in charge of Cook's explorations, employed him to conduct scientific and, in particular, geographic studies of the journey. He had hoped to do more, and later claimed that he had always considered himself as having been sent out primarily to write the history of the voyage. But faced with a cut in his share from the expected profits of the enterprise, he acquiesced and published only scientific material. His son, however, was not satisfied with this state of affairs and decided to publish his own account of the journey around the world.

Johann Georg Adam Forster was only eighteen years old when he joined his father on the Cook expedition, and the second voyage made a great impression on his young inquisitive mind. His acquaintance with Australia was short, in fact he never set foot on the continent and only saw it from a distance, yet he forecast a prominent future for it. 'No part of the world', he wrote, 'so well deserves future investigation as the great continent New Holland, of which we do not know the whole outline, and of whose production we are in a manner entirely ignorant'. And he firmly predicted that 'nothing is more certain . . . than that the inner countries contain immense treasures of natural knowledge, which must of course become of infinite use to the civilised nation which shall first attempt to go in search of them'.[1]

His *Voyage Around the World* was an immediate success. He depicts a paradise, a charming, fascinating world of attractive islands and blue seas. It made the young man famous at the age of twenty-four, and the book's influence is said to have been immense. He was appointed professor at Kassel and Vilna universities, and the popularity of his work opened the door not only to Germany's scholarly community but also to dukes and kings. Even Emperor Joseph II gave the young scientist an audience and listened with interest to Forster's thoughts on the merits of sauerkraut as protection against scurvy. He was in contact with all the great figures of the eighteenth-century German literary scene, including Goethe. In 1788 he became the librarian at the city of Mainz in the southwest of Germany, close to the French border. He was now at the peak of his success. The founder of nineteenth-century exploration, Alexander von Humboldt, dated his interest in the discovery and exploration of nature to his walks with Georg Forster in the lower Rhine region.

The French Revolution of 1789 marked a turning point in Forster's life. His liberal enlightened views became more radical during the course of the revolution and, when French revolutionary forces reached Mainz in October 1792, Forster joined their cause. In fact, he became one of the leading German Jacobins. In March 1793 he addressed the National Convention in Paris to offer a union of the liberated Rhineland with the French Republic. This step soon proved disastrous. Mainz was in due course recaptured by the Prussians and Forster lost all his manuscripts and scientific collections. Worse was to come. He was outlawed by the German governments and a price was put on his head. In France, too, things had taken a turn for the worse. Robespierre's government had taken over from the Girondins and the position of all foreigners had become extremely precarious. One of Forster's friends from Mainz had already been executed. Forster was not immediately threatened – Robespierre even entrusted him with a mission to the north – but his faith in the revolution was fading. He began to doubt whether terror was really the best method of achieving human progress. Forster did not have much time left to ponder this conundrum, which was to trouble revolutionaries and other progressively minded thinkers from then on. He died on 12 January 1794 in Paris – it is believed that his health had been poor since his journey around the world.

Forster may have been disillusioned with the course of the French Revolution, but his faith in a promising future for the newly discovered continent in the Antipodes remained:

New-Holland, an island of immense size . . . will become the future
domicile of a new bourgeois society, which – however insignificant its
beginning seems to be – promises to become soon very important . . .
Indeed the first settlers are a depraved bunch, who in their fatherland
could not be restrained by law nor fear of punishment. Yet the thief is
often the pitiful victim of a useless upbringing, of heartless laws and
inadequate state care [and] past and present history shows that he
stops being an enemy of society once he is granted full human rights
and a property he can till.[2]

Baron Karl Alexander Anselm von Hügel was the first acclaimed
scientist of German-Austrian origin to make a substantial visit to the
Australian continent. A daring adventurer in many ways, he spent
almost a year – November 1833 to October 1834 – traversing what
is now Western Australia, Tasmania and New South Wales. This was
part of a six-year journey covering three continents, during which
he collected 34 000 specimens, from tiny insects to large images of
idols, that he sent to Vienna or brought home with him, in addition to
12 000 pages of diary notes containing minute details of his exploits.

Von Hügel's family came from the town of Koblenz on the Rhine,
where his father was a high-ranking public servant. The very conservative family left the Rhineland in the early 1790s to stay briefly in
Regensburg, where Karl was born in 1795, before settling in Vienna.
Here his father took up a position at the Habsburg Imperial Court and
became, after the defeat of Napoleon, a firm supporter of the Austrian Chancellor Clemens von Metternich, Europe's leading statesman
in the first half of the nineteenth century. Metternich has entered the
history books above all as an ardent reactionary desperately trying to
curb the forces of liberalism and nationalism unleashed by the French
Revolution.

In his early twenties, young Karl was appointed to various diplomatic positions all over Europe, before he settled as a gentleman of
means on the family estate at Hietzing on the outskirts of Vienna.
Here he pursued his interests in the natural sciences, maintaining
large gardens and filling his hothouses with all kinds of exotic plants.
Then private misfortune set in. In 1828 he became engaged to the
beautiful Countess Melanie Zichy Ferraris of an ancient but impoverished Hungarian line. Unfortunately for Karl the young lady called off
the engagement a few months later to marry Metternich (over twenty
years Karl's senior). Heartbroken, he then decided to devote himself
fully to the advancement of natural science. He travelled first to the
Middle East, in particular to Egypt, then to India and Ceylon, from

where he sailed on the British naval frigate *Alligator* to the Swan River colony.

Von Hügel struck it rich in Western Australia, collecting a vast number of plants hitherto unknown in Europe.[3] Here he also seems to have regained his happiness:

> A few hundred paces from the town the vegetation begins and it is a unique thing about the plants of New Holland that their beautiful shapes and the colours of the flowers only become apparent to the observer on closer inspection. Likewise the rich and varied vegetation only appears in its true magnificence when one gets close to it. The unfriendly grey-green turned into a great variety of shades of green, from the brightest and most radiant to the darkest and most succulent interspersed with innumerable shining flowers . . . I wandered about this world as if in a drunken stupor. There was not one plant that I knew . . . For the first time in years, in my long unhappy years, I lived for an hour in the full enjoyment of the moment. In my left hand I held a great bunch of beautiful flowers, while with my right hand I kept picking new species.[4]

From Albany in the southwest von Hügel left for Hobart, where he arrived on 21 January 1834. He spent just a month in Van Diemen's Land, impressed by the cleanliness and decency that for him characterised life in this settlement. He was appalled, however, by the savage treatment meted out to the Aboriginal population, a theme that runs throughout his notes about his stay in Australia. In New South Wales he undertook some risky tours throughout the coastal region and the inland, and again he was impressed. Riding from Maitland to the Hawkesbury River, through Wollombi, he noted:

> for ten miles you have these magnificent flowers constantly before your eyes, and the rocks covered with fern. The rain suddenly came down in such torrents that I simply could not urge my horse forward into it. There were no trees for shelter except an insignificant 'Banksia serrata' which protected my horse rather than me. Suddenly the thick clouds cleared like a veil from the blue sky and the sun lit up the countryside as I approached the last hill. Not for a long time have I seen Nature look more lovely, or seen a more astonishing view.[5]

Von Hügel left Sydney on 6 October 1837 for the Philippines, China and India. Having visited the remote valleys of the Himalayas in Afghanistan, Kashmir and the Punjab, he eventually returned to Vienna in 1837. He was showered with international honours in the following years, including an honorary doctorate of the University of Oxford and the patron's medal by the Royal Geographical Society. When the revolution of 1848 swept Metternich from office, von Hügel rescued him and his wife (the baron's former fiancée) from mob violence in Vienna and, in a daring, adventurous journey, took the couple to England. Apart from the thousands of Australian specimens that he sent or brought home to Vienna, he also left a voluminous edited diary of 2000 pages, handwritten in Gothic script.[6]

There was one more German scientist of note before Ludwig Leichhardt, the most famous of them all, entered the scene. Hessian Johannes Menge was born in 1788 in Steinau and received his education as a mineral collector in neighbouring Hanau. By the 1820s he had established himself as an international mineralogy expert and had set up a successful business in this field in the north German Hanseatic town of Lübeck. He moved to London in the early 1830s, and in 1836 was appointed Mine and Quarry Agent and Geologist in the South Australian Company, the leading force behind the foundation of the colony of South Australia. Menge explored large parts of the north-eastern ranges, especially the Mt Lofty, Mt Barker and Onkaparinga region, and discovered deposits of numerous minerals. However, he did not have the resources to run his own mining enterprise, allegedly because he was seen as an eccentric and is said to have lacked skill in dealing with his fellow men.

He undertook a number of solo explorations stretching over hundreds of kilometres from Cape Jervis to Mt Remarkable, where he made extensive contacts with local Aboriginal tribes, with whom he lived at times. He wrote to a colleague back in Germany:

> Had you seen me now in Australia you would not believe your eyes to see your old friend so ragged, clothes torn, dirty from top to bottom, unshaven with long hair and a long white beard; sleeping in hollow burnt-out trees, or collecting lizards for the black natives, or, to still his hunger after two or three days without foot, demanding roots from them'.[7]

Notwithstanding the fact that he occasionally relieved them of their vegetable roots, he had a fond understanding of their culture, had knowledge of at least three Aboriginal languages and was very critical of white men pushing them off their ancestral lands.

Menge died a pauper on the goldfields in 1852, but many men then and later were making rich pickings from his discoveries around Burra and Kapunda. Although some people thought he was strange, Augustin Lodewyckx – who wrote the first major work on the Germans in Australia – considered him to be the father of South Australian mineralogy.[8]

Ludwig Leichhardt

Ludwig Leichhardt was born on 23 October 1813, the sixth child of the Royal Inspector of Peat, Christian Hyronimus Matthias Leichhardt, and his wife Sophie Charlotte in the village of Trebatsch near the Brandenburg district town of Cottbus. Having attended the local primary school from the age of six to ten, young Ludwig's father, who had recognised his son's talent, arranged for three years of private tuition that prepared him for entry into the Cottbus Grammar School. Three years later his teachers recommended him for admission to the Faculty of Philosophy at Berlin University, which he entered in November 1831. For two years he studied comparative philology, Kantean and Hegelian philosophy and the classics. Following the traditional German practice of rotating universities, Leichhardt enrolled in 1834 for two semesters at the University of Göttingen, where he added biological sciences, mathematics and anatomy.

He returned to Berlin in the spring of 1835 to pursue his doctorate in medicine. There he befriended a young Englishman, William Nicholson, brother of John Nicholson whom Leichhardt had met at Göttingen. William, then also a student of medicine, completed his doctorate in March 1837 and invited his friend to follow him to England. Leichhardt accepted and, having been granted a deferment of Prussian compulsory military service and with permits from his father and the ministry to travel to England, he took up residence with Nicholson's family in Bristol. As his family was very affluent there was no need for William to set up practice immediately, and the two friends decided to pursue their common interest in the natural sciences. In October they went to London, where for the next eight months they worked on collections in the Museum of Natural History, the museum of the Zoological Society and the Royal College of Surgeons. The following June they went to Paris, where they took courses at the Jardin des Plantes and the medical clinic of the Sorbonne. In September 1840 the two students left Paris to tour Italy and Switzerland before returning to England.

Nicholson and Leichhardt now decided to continue their research on – from a European point of view – the recently discovered continent of Australia. But only weeks before the scheduled departure the Englishman pulled out. Family matters prevented him. Nevertheless,

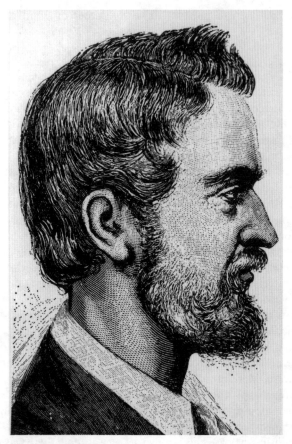

Ludwig Leichhardt

he advanced Leichhardt's fare and lent him £200, so that his friend would not be without means in the strange country. Leichhardt embarked for Australia on 26 October 1841, arriving in Sydney on 14 February 1842. He attempted to find employment as director of the Botanic Gardens. When this failed he undertook scientific reconnaissance work, first around Sydney and, six months later, around Newcastle and the Hunter Valley, before travelling from Port Stephens (north of Newcastle) to Moreton Bay (Brisbane), a distance of nearly 1000 kilometres through what was still almost virgin country. After eighteen months of extensive exploration of the New South Wales coastal regions, he returned to Sydney.[9]

Leichhardt's interest now centred on a new and daring project, which had first been envisaged by the colony's Surveyor General, Sir Thomas Mitchell: to cross the vast northeast of the continent from Moreton Bay via York Peninsula to Port Essington on the northeastern coast of Arnhem Land. It was suggested that he join the expedition, to be led by Mitchell, as a botanist. But preparations were slow, the government would not commit itself to such an expensive venture without the approval of the Legislative Council, and Mitchell himself did not seem to favour undue haste. He was still on an extended holiday in England. Leichhardt became so fascinated by the challenge of such a vast and demanding undertaking that he decided to take the initiative. He enjoyed the support, and indeed in some cases (like William Macarthur) the friendship, of leading and prosperous citizens who contributed to the expedition. However, notwithstanding the generous support of Sydney citizens, the money available to Leichhardt was less than that of government-financed expeditions – such as Mitchell's later Queensland journey of 1845–46.

A stringent budget allowed for a party of only 9 men, 16 cattle, 17 horses and 4 dogs. On 1 October 1844 they set out. The terrain was not easy but no heavy rain fell until well into December, and even then it was not sustained. The Aborigines they met were friendly and curious. All this allowed for good mileage on most days. By the middle of January 1845 the party reached a river they named the Mackenzie and, a few days later, the Peak Ranges. In February the summer heat hit the expedition and the diaries recorded regular and extensive searches for water. In early April they reached the Burdekin River, named after one of the Sydney benefactors. On 23 May they reached the Lund River. By now they had run out of virtually all their provisions, and Leichhardt wrote to his brother-in-law:

> As I never thought that the journey would take so long, our provisions did not last. We went for seven months without flour, much longer without sugar, several months without salt, and finally ran out of tea, so that we were reduced to nothing but dried beef. It was the dried beef that enabled me to complete the journey.[10]

A fatal disaster struck the party on 28 June 1845, when their camp was attacked by Aborigines. There has always been – and still is – considerable disagreement about the reasons for the attack. Traditional accounts maintained that it occurred because the two Aboriginal members of the party had tried to become too intimate with some of the tribeswomen, but recent scholarship repudiates this interpretation.

Colin Roderick, who wrote the latest and most up-to-date biography of Leichhardt, claims that the party was attacked because they camped on a sacred ceremonial ground. Brian Dalton, another Leichhardt scholar, argues that a punishment party had gathered in response to the collection of a sacred waterlily. Yet another explanation has been advanced by Fred Rose, formerly Professor of Anthropology at Leipzig University, who lived for several years in the 1930s among the Aborigines. Rose claims that the attack occurred close to the place where Dutch sailors at the beginning of the previous century had landed and killed several tribesmen when attempting to abduct them. According to Rose, this encounter became part of Aboriginal folk memory and the attack on Leichhardt's party must be seen as an act of revenge. Whatever the cause, the result was fatal. The naturalist John Gilbert was killed and two others injured, although not severely. Their wounds were tended by Leichhardt, whose medical knowledge was of great assistance.

The remainder of the journey was marked by fatigue and exhaustion. The countryside, which was at times tropical and at times arid, was taking its toll. By now, a year after they had set out from Moreton Bay, they were getting on each other's nerves, and when they finally ran into a group of Aborigines who greeted them with 'Aye Aye, Sir' (a sign that their goal was within striking distance), few words could describe their relief. On 17 December, after a journey that had lasted fourteen and a half months, they stumbled into Port Essington. They took a schooner a month later, and arrived back in Sydney on 24 March 1846.

A tumultuous welcome greeted the heroes of what was then the longest and most daring exploration in the history of European settlement in Australia. The explorers were richly rewarded, and the lion's share went to Leichhardt. Few apart from a handful of detractors doubted that he deserved most of the credit for the successful undertaking.

Leichhardt enjoyed his immense popularity. It would have been easy for him to take up a lucrative position, rest on his laurels, and enjoy the friendship of a lady companion. References to women are not uncommon in his letters and diaries. In fact he fell in love twice during his time in Sydney, first with Marianne Marlow (eldest daughter of Captain Marlow of the Royal Engineers), and later with Emmeline Macarthur (daughter of Hannibal Hawkins Macarthur). But Leichhardt did not settle down to domestic life. The sensation caused by his first successful expedition had hardly abated when he was already preparing for his life's mission: to cross the continent from east to west and thus solve the great mystery of the Australian interior.

It took him only six months to set up his second expedition. He sank all his rewards from the successful Port Essington venture into the enterprise, and again managed to raise funds from benefactors. Leichhardt's team consisted of three gentlemen, Henry Matthew Turnbull, John Mann and Hovenden Hely; three 'working men'; Daniel Bunce, James Perry and the expedition's cook, Henry Boecking – also a German. Finally, there were two Aborigines: Wommai and Brown. Compared to the Port Essington journey, supplies were lavish – but then Leichhardt estimated that the crossing would take between two-and-a-half and three years. They took 15 mules, 14 horses, 270 goats, 108 sheep and 40 cattle. On 10 December 1846 they set out on an expedition that from the very beginning was visited by every conceivable misfortune.

Men who were sent after Leichhardt to inform him of Sir Thomas Mitchell's unsuccessful attempt to reach Port Essington, and who were to pass on valuable information gathered by him, failed to reach the party. Then came rain. Torrential downpours turned dry creeks into huge flooded rivers. With the rain came myriad insects. Soon everybody was suffering from fever and other illnesses. When they reached the Mackenzie River, floodwaters prevented them from crossing for three weeks. When finally they did reach the other bank, the most severe bout of fever so far affected the whole team, forcing a further rest of three weeks. Mules, cattle and horses constantly broke their hobbles and, with the exception of Leichhardt and Wommai, there were few capable hands to round them up again. Leichhardt managed to persuade his team to push a last desperate 110 kilometres and reach the foot of the Peak Ranges. By now they had lost their sheep and goats, and the cattle had broken loose again.

Sensing that failure was inevitable Leichhardt, in despair and disappointment, blamed some of his men. They were young and inexperienced, they were not made for the hardship the expedition entailed. He called to mind his first team of men – he had obviously forgotten how he had cursed them in letters written on their way back from Port Essington to Sydney. He recalled how those men were eating goannas, possums, parrots and crows by the time they reached the Mackenzie River. Kangaroo meat had been a luxury. On this journey, they had been slaughtering a sheep per day, and Leichhardt felt that the constant diet of mutton was the reason for their poor constitutions and frequent illnesses. Recent research has confirmed that it was a badly regulated diet and that unhygienic slaughtering methods caused the constant bouts of fever and other illnesses.[11] Now that all the sheep were lost they were forced to eat dried beef: perhaps this change of diet might provide them with the necessary strength to continue. Alas, it did not. The team grew ever weaker, and the constant rain made it hard to dry the beef. Finally, they lost their cattle for good. On 7 June 1847 Leichhardt announced to his team that they would return.

There is some justification for Leichhardt's claim that he was let down by some of his men. From the evidence available Hely and Mann, in particular, seem to have lacked the stamina for such a demanding expedition. But it also seems that given the adverse weather conditions and their disastrous consequences, no team, whatever its skills and powers of endurance, would have succeeded at that particular time. The decision to return brought sudden and speedy recovery all round, and within six weeks they were back in the Darling Downs. Acrimonious quarrels broke out among the party once they were back in civilisation, and the public soon lost interest in the buck-passing.

Leichhardt was not despondent, and immediately started new preparations. After six months he was ready to resume his attempt to reach the Indian Ocean. Several of his old party offered to accompany him but, perhaps because he thought this a bad omen or because he was convinced that the team had let him down, he recruited a new group of men. In March 1848 he set out with 7 men, 20 mules, 7 horses and 50 cattle. He was confident, but also knew to be careful:

> as I have taken all the precautions my experience suggested we have travelled without any accident at least these 80 miles. My mules are in good order and my cattle are very quiet. One of the greatest difficulties I always had to fight with was to keep the backs of my animals sound, and to keep them in good steady travelling train. To effect this I have paid great attention to the saddles and have put strong leather halters on each of them by which I am enabled to rein them up and to prevent them from feeding during the journey. For if allowed to feed, they try to run ahead to obtain a few moments to take a bite and consequently they break their steady step which is the principal cause of their sore backs. I cannot speak in too high terms of my present party, who seem to me well qualified for the long and tedious journey which is before us.[12]

On 1 April 1848 he wrote his last letter to his old friend, Captain Phillip Parker King. He was in a buoyant mood. Everything was proceeding smoothly; he felt certain of success this time. But this was the last time the party was seen or heard from.

The disappearance of Leichhardt in his second attempt to cross the continent from east to west fascinated his contemporaries for many decades. A first expedition to search for the missing party set out in January 1852 under Hovenden Hely. It discovered tent-poles that may well have been left by Leichhardt, and trees with the letter 'L' and 'XVA' engraved at the upper Warrego River, but was otherwise unsuccessful. Charles Gregory started a new search in July 1855, which began from a base camp set up at the mouth of the Victoria River. Attempts to find clues to the west or south of the camp were unsuccessful but, after travelling 400 kilometres east, Gregory discovered a creek (today's Elsey Creek) where trees had been cut with European axes. There were also traces of abandoned huts built by white men, and of wooden cups. As no other European team had been in the region, this could only point to the presence of the Leichhardt expedition. Further searches over several decades located more 'L' trees, pieces of leather belts, European clothes and blankets, white people's skeletons and imprints of horses, mules and oxen in country that no Europeans other than the Leichhardt team had traversed. John McDouall Stuart, in his south–north crossing of 1861–62, even came across Aboriginal people who knew the Freemason symbol (Leichhardt was a Freemason) – and on the return leg, again in a region where only the Leichhardt expedition could have been, he noticed a young part-white, part-Aboriginal boy, aged about twelve.

To his credit, Bernd Marx, a keen Leichhardt scholar who is today in charge of the Leichhardt Museum in Trebatsch, put all these pieces together and sketched the likely route of the last expedition. Marx believes that Leichhardt was heading northwest again, towards the Gulf of Carpentaria, and that he was travelling further inland than his first expedition, though keeping well north of the Simpson Desert. Most likely, the team then went to Port Essington again, to rest and to replenish their resources. But the settlement had been abandoned in 1849, and hence their efforts were in vain. It is not idle to speculate that without new supplies Leichhardt realised he could not continue his east–west crossing and decided to head for the 'red centre' – another goal he had set himself. The expedition then probably went south as far as Central Mt Stuart (near today's Tennant Creek) before turning southeast towards civilisation. All evidence points to the men being attacked at the Wantata waterhole near Coopers Creek, 200 kilometres east of what is today the small settlement of Bedourie. All but one white member of the party was killed.[13]

Already a legend in his own lifetime, Leichhardt passed into Australian mythology after his disappearance. Along with others such as Sturt, Eyre, Stuart and A. C. Gregory, he ranks among the leading nineteenth-century European explorers of the continent. Contemporaries ranked his work highly, and not only in Australia. For his considerable contribution to botany, zoology, geology and medicine, he received major awards from London, Paris and even his native Prussia. The few later attempts to belittle his achievements were unconvincing.[14] In Australia, Leichhardt is a household word today. Towns and plants, highways, streets, suburbs, electorates, schools, parks, hotels and motels carry his name.

In Germany – strange, given the fact that this country produced few explorers of international acclaim – the opposite is the case. Before reunification, students of English literature in the former Federal Republic (West Germany) may have come across his name while studying the novel *Voss* by the Australian winner of the Nobel Prize for Literature, Patrick White – although the novel has little to do with the explorer. In the Democratic Republic (the former East Germany), of which Leichhardt's homeland Brandenburg became part after the division of Germany, the situation was more promising. Here, an active group of *Leichhardtianer* managed against difficult odds to establish a formidable record of memorabilia collections, publications, exhibitions and lectures. After reunification, a Leichhardt year with many guest lecturers was held in 1999 in the Brandenburg capital, Potsdam, and other locations in the state. There was even a stage production mounted in memory of the explorer by high school students in Cottbus, the district capital.[15]

Today there is little interest in the explorer in Australia's German community. In September 2004 five Queensland shires, all situated in 'Leichhardt country', held a large 'Expo' to honour one of Australia's most famous explorers. The interest of the German communities and officials was minimal, and German-language newspapers drew attention to the event only in the form of paid advertisements. Likewise, a huge advertising campaign in Germany brought no results.

Ludwig Leichhardt was the most famous explorer of German origin to perish while challenging the vastness of the Australian continent, but he was not the only one. Ludwig Becker, one of the three Germans in the team that accompanied Burke and Wills in their attempted south–north crossing of the continent in 1860–61, was the third member of that equally ill-fated expedition to suffer a tragic death.[16] The other two Germans were the expedition's doctor, Hermann Beckler, who resigned because he could not endure the manner in which Burke was conducting the expedition, and Alexander Brahe, who gave the fatal order on 21 April 1861 to return to Menindee only hours before Burke, Wills and King reached the depot at Coopers Creek.

Ferdinand von Mueller

Unlike Leichhardt, Becker and some other explorers, Baron Sir Ferdinand Jakob Heinrich von Mueller survived his explorations and died in a hospital bed of a stroke on 10 October 1896, at the age of seventy-one. Although he achieved much, he was almost always lonely and disappointed. Mueller's home was Schleswig-Holstein in northern Germany. Both his parents died of tuberculosis during his childhood, which left him with a constant fear that he too might die from this illness. To live in a climate less conducive to tuberculosis was the main reason why Ferdinand and his two sisters, Bertha and Clara, moved to Australia, arriving in Adelaide in December 1847. Mueller had already received his degree in pharmacology from Kiel University, and a short time later his thesis on the common herb, shepherd's purse (*Capsella bursa-pastoris*), was accepted and he was awarded a doctorate.

After a few years in the South Australian capital, Mueller went to Melbourne, where Governor Charles La Trobe appointed him the colony's botanist in 1853. It was during the 1850s that he undertook most of his explorations. His first journey, from February to April 1853, was with John Dallachy, a Scotsman from Morayshire who had only recently been appointed Curator of Melbourne's Botanic Gardens. The two men travelled to the Victorian Alps and the Ovens Valley. They climbed Mt Buffalo and were the first to ascend Mt Aberdeen, later renamed Mt Wilson. Dallachy had to return to his duties in Melbourne but Mueller continued his exploration. Then followed two more journeys, this time alone, to the Victorian Alps and the Snowy Mountains, to undertake further botanical investigations. He climbed Mt Kosciuszko just after New Year's Day 1855 and on his return claimed that he had documented most specimens of the alpine flora. Travelling to the high country remained a favourite activity, and in subsequent years Mueller continued to visit the Snowy Mountains, usually accompanied by friends. Ludwig Becker, for example, was one of his companions, as was the Director of the Victorian National School of Art, Austrian Eugene von Guérard.

Mueller's achievements were widely recognised, and in 1855 he was appointed botanist to the northwestern expedition under A. C. Gregory. This expedition, which attempted among other things to find traces of Leichhardt's expedition, lasted for sixteen months and covered a distance of 8000 kilometres – from the Victoria River to the Joseph Bonaparte Gulf (near today's border between Western Australia and the Northern Territory) and from there to Moreton Bay. The expedition was very successful. Mueller managed to collect nearly 2000 species, of which 800 were new to European botanical science. This opened up many opportunities for him. He was invited by Sir William Hooker to come to the Royal Botanic Gardens at Kew in London, and powerful friends in England promised him a brilliant career. However, for reasons not altogether discernible, Mueller did not leave Melbourne. He was to stay in Australia for the rest of his life. In 1857 he took up the directorship of the Botanic Gardens, in addition to his position as Government Botanist. He was a relentless worker and in subsequent years earned countless titles and honours.

His major works were the 12-volume *Fragmenta Phytographiae*, the 7-volume *Flora Australiensis* and *Eucalyptographia: A Descriptive Atlas of the Eucalypts of Australia and the Adjoining Islands*, which appeared over ten decades. He published another seven books and a string of articles on such diverse subjects as rust in cereals and the culture of tea in Victoria, to the advancement of the natural sciences by clergymen. His correspondence is said to have sometimes reached 3000 letters per annum, all of which he replied to in his own hand. All told, more than 2000 Australian plants were first ascribed to him. Herbariums all around the world received an enormous number of dried plants; the Royal Bavarian Herbarium at Munich alone is said to have received up to 600 species of Australian plants. This was only the beginning:

He succeeded in sending the 8,000 lbs [3.6 tonnes] meteor found in Western Port, to the British Museum. The Senckenberg Scientific Society at Frankfurt/Main owes him gratitude for the fish Ceratodus, which at the time was one of the greatest rarities in European museums. Von Mueller presented to the Königlich-Württembergisches Naturalienkabinett at Stuttgart 2,269 vertebrates belonging to 837 species and a great number of invertebrates. The Botanical Gardens in Europe were able to extend their collection with the help of many seeds sent by Mueller at regular intervals. He also sent to Europe valuable living plants. In 1888 the Botanical Garden of Dresden received from him, as a gift, an enormous Todea barbata plant weighing 6 hundred-weight [300 kilograms] and belonging to the king ferns, which in its new home soon started to sprout and brought forth a leaf crown of 120 fronds. It was taken from a forest valley of Victoria on a carriage drawn by ten oxen. This was already the eighth exemplar he had given to European gardens. One exemplar of a Todea given by him to the Botanical Garden at Munich was estimated to be worth 200 Marks in the currency of that time. An announced delivery of Dicksonia trunks, which soon brought forth an imposing little tree-fern wood in the cold-house, arrived in Dresden in good time in 1889. Mueller himself undertook to pay for the certainly not inexpensive freight costs up to the German reception harbour! The greatest Todea, weighing 4,800 kg, 7 inches wide and high [sic] went to St. Petersburg. The government had brought this fern over 100 miles to Melbourne using twelve oxen. For this transport, some special bridges had to be built in various places. Eucalyptus plantations in Italy, Southern France, India, South Africa and North America were cultivated for draining swamps and fast wood-production initially on the recommendation of Mueller as were the acacia woods in South Africa, Ceylon and India. The Riviera horticulture owes its fortune, above all, to Ferdinand Mueller who played a great part in introducing acacias, proteaceas and myrtaceas, which were very popular winter flowers at that time.[17]

Mueller also was a member of 150 learned societies, in almost every country of the globe. In Melbourne, he was the founder or co-founder of the Royal Society of Victoria, the Acclimatisation Society, the Zoological Society, the Horticultural Society, the Pharmaceutical Society and the Field Naturalists' Club. He was also the President of the Royal Geographical Society (Victorian Branch), a fellow of the Linnean Society, and of the Royal Societies in London, New South Wales and Tasmania. In 1871 the King of Württemberg made him a hereditary baron. In 1868 Queen Victoria made him a Companion of the Order of St Michael, and in 1879 a Knight Commander of the Order of St Michael and St George. The French emperor Napoleon III appointed him a Knight of the Legion of Honour and he received decorations from many European states, including a medal from the Royal Society in London.

But all these achievements and honours failed to bring him sat-isfaction and happiness. In 1873 von Mueller became the victim of petty colonial politics and was dismissed from the directorship of the Botanic Gardens. There were not enough flowers, it was said; the gar-den did not portray the prosperity of a metropolis such as marvellous

Baron Sir Ferdinand von Mueller

Melbourne. Although he kept his position as Government Botanist and he suffered no pecuniary losses, the loss of the directorship was a severe personal blow to von Mueller, from which he never recovered. The gardens had filled some of the empty spaces in his life, a compensation for his lack of closeness to other people. He never enjoyed an intimate friendship or a deep personal relationship. The directorship had meant more than position, prestige and honour, and as one of his biographers aptly comments, 'the price of eminence was high. He had become more a botanist than a man.'[18] Because of these great achievements, von Mueller has at times been compared to the German polymath Alexander von Humboldt: indeed, the leading German nineteenth-century geographer August Petermann referred to him as the Humboldt of Australia.

They came and they went

The list of German scientists who came to Australia during the nineteenth century and left after shorter or longer scientific exploits is long. Relations between most German states (and after 1871 the German Empire) and the United Kingdom, together with its colonies in the Antipodes, remained amicable for most of the century. And as German universities had taken the lead in many scientific fields, it was only natural that the newly discovered continent would attract major attention. Astronomer and marine scientist Christian Karl Ludwig Rümker arrived in 1821 to take charge of Governor Sir Thomas Macdougall Brisbane's private observatory at Parramatta. He was appointed Government Astronomer (and given 1000 acres of land) as reward for his rediscovery of the 'Encke-planet'. Although he was granted further generous land allocations, he returned to Hamburg in 1830 to take over the directorship of the Hamburg School of Navigation. Prague-born Franz Wilhelm Sieber was the first German botanist to collect Australian plants. He arrived in Sydney in 1823, stayed for seven months, and left with 300 collected plants.

Botanist and naturalist Johann Ludwig Preiss, from the Harz mountain region of Germany, arrived in the Swan River colony in 1838 and is accredited with having compiled the most extensive collection of botanical and zoological specimens ever in Western Australia. He tried to establish German emigration to the colony, but was thwarted by the British government.[19] Also in Western Australia, geologist Ferdinand von Sommer from Göttingen was employed by the government in 1847 to search for mineral and coal deposits. He surveyed the region around Irwin River (towards today's Geraldton) and Cape Naturaliste in the south, went as far east as Doubtful Island and Bremer Bay, and inland to the Stirling Range. The government, however, was not satisfied with his efforts and he returned to Germany in 1848.

Before the age of the camera, painters and illustrators were very important members of exploratory expeditions and Germans seemed to have been a popular choice. Josef Albert Franz David Herrgott, who was born in Bavaria in 1825, came to Australia during the early gold rush days. His skills as bushman, naturalist and artist soon led him to join a number of expeditions that were arranged and financed by the South Australian government. He took part in B. H. Babbage's expedition to Lake Torrens in 1858. Herrgott's humorous sketches of this expedition can be viewed today in the library of the South Australian branch of the Royal Geographical Society of Australasia. In 1859 he joined John McDouall Stuart's second expedition to explore the country between Lake Torrens and Lake Eyre. It was Herrgott who found the springs that were named after him, to the southeast of Lake Eyre South. The small settlement that soon grew near the springs – at what was to become the southern end of the Birdsville track – was also named Herrgott's Springs, but following World War I was renamed Marree.

Herrgott became joint leader in an attempt later in 1859 by Alexander Tolmer, one of the less-well-known explorers of South Australia, to undertake the south-north crossing. This expedition ended in complete failure. Herrgott died two years later, only 36 years old. He was warmly remembered, as is shown by this obituary in an Adelaide newspaper:

> The deceased was a native of Bavaria; but was thoroughly conversant with French and English, as to locality, manners, and language. His general attainments in the arts and sciences were of no ordinary character, and he has left behind him many a trace of his mastery in nature and art. As a citizen of the world, he was just, frank, manly; as a friend he was intelligent, generous, kind; and his premature exit into the spirit world is deplored by a large circle of friends, both German and English.[20]

Georg Baltasar Neumayer was born at Kirchheimbolanden in the Bavarian Palatinate in 1826 and studied a series of scientific disciplines, in particular physics and astronomy at Munich University, before being appointed to a chair of physics at Hamburg University. He first came to Australia in 1852, and worked for two years on the goldfields of Bendigo. On his return to Germany he managed to attract enough interest as well as financial backing for his plan to set up a physical observatory in Melbourne for the study of terrestrial magnetic and related phenomena. After initial difficulties with the colonial government, he succeeded in setting up an astronomical observatory on Flagstaff Hill in 1858, and a second one near the Botanic Gardens in 1862–64. He conducted extensive magnetic and meteorological observations and also completed, virtually single-handedly, a thorough magnetic survey of Victoria. To do this he travelled some 18 000 kilometres on foot, with a packhorse, and set up magnetic stations from sea level to an altitude of about 2200 metres. He returned to Germany in 1864, where his impressive career culminated in the directorship of the Hamburg Oceanic Observatory. He is remembered above all for his encouragement of the scientific exploration of the Antarctic region, which commenced on a grand scale in the twentieth century.

*Georg von Neumayer's second observatory on the left bank of the Yarra River
(Georg von Neumayer Collection, Pfalzmuseum für Naturkunde, Pollichia-
Museum, Bad Dürkheim)*

William Blandowski arrived in Australia in 1849, and after brief
stays in Adelaide and Sydney made a small fortune on the Victorian
goldfields – where he was noted as the inventor and designer of a
powerful water pump. In 1852 he settled in Melbourne where, a year
later, he founded the Geological Society of Victoria, and in 1854 he
was appointed Government Zoologist to the newly created Museum
of Natural History. In December 1856 the Victorian government
appointed him leader of an expedition to investigate the flora and fauna
around the junction of the Darling and Murray rivers. Aided by Johann
Ludwig Krefft, another German naturalist, and having overcome many
physical challenges, his collection of 17 400 specimens filled 28 boxes.
He returned to Melbourne in September 1857, and the rest of his
stay was marred by continuous confrontations with Professor Frederick McCoy who, against Blandowski's will, had transferred specimens
from the museum to the University of Melbourne. Blandowski refused
to hand over part of his collection and, when threatened with legal
action, left Australia to return to his native Silesia in 1859. His assistant in the 1857 Murray/Darling expedition became curator of the
Australian Museum in Sydney in 1864 and built up a spectacular collection. An outstanding zoologist of international repute, he too fell
out with – and was dismissed by – the colonial government.[21]

Robert Ignaz Lendlmayer von Lendenfeld from Graz in Austria was a biologist and keen alpinist (he had several first ascents in the Austrian Alps to his credit). He lived in Australia and New Zealand with his wife for four-and-a-half years (1881–85), mainly lecturing at technical and agricultural colleges. Under contract to the Sydney Museum, von Lendenfeld studied Australian sponges and jellyfish. He too travelled widely through the Australian and New Zealand Alps, where he was the first to notice that the mountain the Polish explorer Strzelecki had named Kosciuszko, and claimed to be the highest peak in Australia, was in fact 26 metres lower than the neighbouring Mt Townsend.[22]

The list of nineteenth-century German scientists coming to Australia could be multiplied,[23] but this chapter concludes with a brief reference to Amalia Dietrich, acclaimed as one of the most important naturalists to have worked in Australia. Dietrich spent ten years of her life, from 1863 to 1872, in Queensland collecting anthropological, botanical, ethnological and zoological specimens for the private museum of her employer, the Hamburg shipowner J. C. Godeffroy. She was born in Siebenlehen (Saxony) in 1821, the daughter of a glove- and purse-maker. Her interest in the natural sciences began with her marriage to Wilhelm Dietrich, a natural scientist who earned his living through the collection and sale of insect, amphibian and reptile specimens. She worked with him for several years, collecting and preparing natural history specimens throughout Europe but, disillusioned with his infidelity, left her husband in 1861. Amalia continued to work as a specimen collector to eke out a meagre income for herself and her daughter, the only child of her marriage.

In 1863 Godeffroy offered Dietrich a contract to collect natural history specimens in Australia, and she gladly accepted, even though this meant leaving her daughter to the care of relatives. Dietrich's travels in remote parts of Queensland were as daring and demanding as those of any of her male counterparts and the product of her work was immense. She is said to have compiled the largest collections of birds ever made by a single person, to have made the first significant collection of Australian spiders and to have gathered some of Australia's deadliest snakes. In the country around Bowen she worked for three years to amass a vast number of Aboriginal items: clubs, spears, canoes, fishing nets and hooks, skeletons and skulls were all sent to Hamburg.

It was her dealings with Aborigines that cast a dark shadow over her reputation. The story goes that Dietrich, while a guest at the estate

Amalia Dietrich

of the Archer family outside Rockhampton, asked an employee to go out and shoot an Aborigine for her so that she could have the skin mounted for display in Germany. William Archer, who held a strong interest in Aboriginal culture, is said to have ordered that she be driven back to town immediately. The fact that the Zoological Museum in Hamburg later displayed the tanned skin of an Australian Aborigine collected by Dietrich seems to verify the allegation. Whether the claim that shooting Aborigines was common practice in Queensland at that time – if correct – provides mitigating circumstances is debatable.

After ten years in the Australian bush, Dietrich returned to Germany an eccentric figure, shabby in her appearance and with rough mannerisms, an embarrassment to her daughter – who had been educated at her mother's expense at a private boarding school. Dietrich lived for a few years in a flat provided by her employer, but when the Godeffroy company went bankrupt she was moved to a home for elderly women, where she died in 1891. Dietrich achieved fame posthumously not because of her outstanding scientific collection but because of her 'biography', published by her daughter Charitas. The book, which gained wide circulation, presents an enviable heroine, a woman of boundless energy defying fate in the most dangerous environments, living a simple, unpretentious life, and toiling laboriously for little reward. It turned out that the letters – allegedly written by Amalia to her daughter – upon which the book was based were fraudulent. Not long ago a more honest biographer did not hesitate to rank her as an exceptional woman and a great naturalist.[24]

4
MISSIONARIES

Interpretations of the work of Christian missionaries among the Aboriginal people vary greatly. On the positive side, those with strong Christian beliefs consider that saving a number of 'savages' from eternal damnation justifies the huge costs of the enterprise, in terms of both human lives and enormous material effort. For others, the missionaries at least came to the assistance of the Indigenous people at a time when support and care were desperately needed and helpers were few and far between. Then there are historians who argue that the missionaries were blinded by their religious beliefs, and that their relentless attempts to convert the 'heathens' to the true faith did as much to uproot the local tribes as did those who ruthlessly forced people off their native lands or destroyed them with the bottle. And finally, in the current Australian 'history wars' and 'frontier wars' controversy, there is the Keith Windschuttle school of thought, which condemns the missionaries for having forced the Aborigines into reserves or other forms of closed settlements, away from the mainstream of society, and so impeded the process of integration into the new Australia which, allegedly, was what most of them wanted. German missionaries were among the most active, not hesitating to venture into the most remote and – from a European point of view – most hostile parts of the continent. Their story might shed light on the controversy.

In the century before World War I, missionary activity was a huge enterprise in Europe – and nowhere more so than in the German-speaking lands. Twenty-six evangelical (i.e. Lutheran or United) missionary training centres alone were established during the nineteenth century. According to the 1910 mission statistics, they maintained

670 *Hauptstationen* (main-stations) and 3150 *Nebenstationen* (out-stations or sub-stations) overseas. There were 1065 ordained mission-aries, 19 mission medical practitioners, 223 lay helpers, 194 mission sisters and 6377 'native helpers' or mission workers. There were said to be 565 000 'heathen Christians' and a further 256 000 entitled to take Holy Communion.[1] If to this we add the Catholic mission-aries and the missionary activities of other non-Lutheran Protestant denominations, in particular the Pietists, then the dimensions of the missionary enterprise become clear. Missionising Australia was part of this enterprise from the early decades of the nineteenth century, and it was apparent from the start that the task of converting the Aboriginal people to Christianity would be a difficult one – meeting with far fewer 'successes' than in Africa, India or parts of the Pacific Islands. All ini-tial attempts – of which none managed to last longer than a decade – failed.

The first record of German missionary activities in the Antipodes has been traced back to 1831, when Johann Christian Simon Handt went with his wife to what is today the Wellington region of New South Wales. Johann, however, soon fell very ill and the couple returned to Sydney. Subsequent attempts were similarly unsuccessful. The Reverend J. Dunmore Lang, one of the most energetic entrepreneurs of early white Australia, was the motor behind the establishment of the Gossner Mission at Moreton Bay in 1838. Zion's Hill, now the north Brisbane suburb of Nundah, became the first free settle-ment in Queensland. Lang recruited Reverend Carl Wilhelm Schmidt, an ordained minister of the Prussian United Church, and Reverend Christoph Eipper from Esslingen in Württemberg, a graduate of the Lutheran Missionary College at Basle, to work among the Indige-nous tribes of the area around Brisbane and the Bunya Mountains. They were later joined by Pastors J. G. Hausmann, W. Gericke and J. P. Niguet, but their efforts, too, met with repeated setbacks and the station was closed on order of the government in 1846.[2]

Also in 1838, the Dresden Mission Society sent two missionaries, C. W. Schürmann and C. G. Teichelmann, to South Australia to work among the Aborigines in the vicinities of Adelaide, Port Lincoln and Encounter Bay. Two more clergymen followed in 1840. Again they had no success in converting the heathen but by 1846 had managed to publish four pamphlets on Aboriginal languages and customs. Lack of finances put an end to their enterprise and they became pastors in Fritzsche's Evangelical Church. Their work is credited with having led to a change in policy towards Aborigines. Instead of 'assimilation' there was now to be 'assimilation after segregation': efforts must first be concentrated on settling 'the natives' on a mission station, away from the influences of other Aboriginal groups and of dissolute whites.

Most active among the missionaries were the Bohemian and Moravian brothers. Their long series of attempts to establish mission stations in Australia – there were seven altogether, some of which did achieve longevity – began at Lake Boga, 300 kilometres northwest of Melbourne (near today's Swan Hill) in 1851.[3] After five fruitless years, this project is said to have been wrecked by government indifference and the greed of local squatters.[4] But it was the Hermannsburg mission stations in the torrid conditions of central Australia that attracted the fascination of both contemporaries and later chroniclers.

Holy Hermannsburg

The Hermannsburger Missionsanstalt was founded by the brothers Louis and Theodor Harms – both ardent Christians – in 1849 in the village of Hermannsburg, in what was then the Kingdom of Hanover and is today Lower Saxony. Hermannsburg was reputed to be a particularly devout Christian community and, according to the Missionsanstalt's chronicler, Louis, the elder of the two brothers, took the initiative because 'he felt pity in his heart for the poorest of the poor, the heathens; and a sense of guilt for not having done anything so far to contribute to their salvation tortured his soul and urged him to act'.[5] Over the years, one thousand missionaries, accompanied by a large number of lay staff called *Kolonisten* (colonists), set out from here to spread the gospel among the heathens of the globe.

Admission to the college was simple, and there was never any shortage of keen candidates. A missionary trainee (*Zögling*) had to be aged between twenty-two and twenty-five, and be free from military obligation. *Zöglinge* also needed parental permission, because Louis Harms firmly believed that 'only with the blessings of the parents can one serve the Master among the heathens' and he rejected applications that did not show full parental support. Above all, would-be trainees had to be fully dedicated to the cause of the Lord and the (true) Lutheran confession. Probably because they felt that it was easier to mould 'simple' uneducated young men than university-trained candidates, the Harms brothers preferred people with peasant and artisan backgrounds to trained theologians with tertiary education. Whereas the missionaries were to be in charge of the spiritual part of the enterprise, the colonists were to look after the everyday tasks of running the station.

Mission stations were expected to be virtually self-supporting and, if possible, to make a modest profit from crops or livestock to meet the many expenditures. However, there were no rules or guidelines to establish a clear dividing line between the functions of the missionaries and the colonists. Certainly the missionaries had to participate in the construction and maintenance of the station, in particular during its early stages, and although the colonists could not provide proper church services in the form of sermons or baptisms, they always had to set an example by living an upright Christian life, and were obliged to undertake minor church duties such as preparatory Bible classes. Naturally, young men who wanted to become *Kolonisten* had to be firm Lutherans, but they did not have to go through the thorough theological training of the missionaries.

A third group in the missionary process did not figure prominently in the preparations but was as important to the enterprise as the missionaries and *Kolonisten*: the women. The Lutheran Church, in stark contrast to Catholicism, firmly believed that pastors should be married and set an example to their congregation by living a pious family life. Missionaries were expected to marry as soon as possible, because this would give them further strength in an often hostile environment. Marriages were often – though not always – arranged. Young women from Hermannsburg and surrounding parishes, if they had strong enough religious conviction and the courage to live far from home (or perhaps if they had begun to fear that time was running out for them to find a fit local suitor), soon found themselves at sea, heading for distant shores.

The Harms-run enterprise was very successful. After a decade and a half they had already sent over one hundred trained missionaries, accompanied by wives and colonists, to Africa and the Indian subcontinent, and they had every reason to be satisfied with their achievements. But pleasing as their successes were, it began to appear that there was a price to pay for them. The enterprise had grown so large that problems were inevitable. Difficulties and disagreements with people sent abroad seemed to be increasing, especially the development of 'unionist tendencies' in missionaries in Africa, which soon spread to India. Moreover, Louis' enormous dedication to his cause was taking its physical toll. His health was steadily deteriorating. He began to feel that emphasis should be on consolidation rather than growth. Thus, not surprisingly, when he received a letter from South Australia asking for missionaries to work among the Aborigines in the Lake Eyre region, Harms's first reaction was anything but excited. He wrote to a friend in Pittsburgh, USA:

Our dear mission enterprise is flourishing under God's blessing, yet, looking at myself, I feel despondent. In addition to the work in Africa and India . . . I have been asked to send missionaries to New Holland. They expect them already at *Michaelis* (Michelmas), this is almost too much for my limited strength.

Yet, if God called upon him, he felt obliged to obey. Louis' forebodings proved right. Arranging the departure of missionaries to South Australia was his last achievement.[6]

The first Hermannsburg missionaries in Australia

Few places targeted for mission work could match the physical challenge posed by the arid conditions of the first stations founded – and initially run – by Hermannsburg missionaries and their wives, colonists and helpers. Their efforts were marked by almost continuous disappointment and disaster.

The first group to leave Germany to take up duties in Australia embarked at Hamburg on 6 May 1866. The small community was made up of two pastors, George Heidenreich and Christian Hellmut, and their families; two missionaries, Ernst Homann and Johann Gössling; and the *Kolonist* Hermann Vogelsang. The missionaries had been ordained only two months earlier, and their farewell service at Hermannsburg church on Easter Sunday had been a particularly sad one because of the recent death of the station's founding father. The new head of the Hermannsburger Missionsanstalt, Louis' brother Theodor, gave the sermon, in which he reminded the young missionaries of the difficult task they faced in trying to convert the 'Papua' who, according to the younger Harms, were among the most depraved people on earth. He claimed that they knew 'neither laws, nor right or wrong', and were a nomadic people who ate not only 'worms, snakes, carrion and raw meat but also the flesh of their slain enemies and their own children'. However, the missionaries could take comfort in knowing that they were guided and protected by their saviour.[7]

The group arrived in South Australia in August 1866 and spent the next few weeks busily visiting the numerous Lutheran churches and their congregations, meeting and mingling with the German communities – who left no doubt that they were greatly excited about the arrival from Hermannsburg. The Lutherans in the Barossa Valley, on hearing the news of Stuart's successful south–north crossing of the continent, and that thousands of natives in the north were waiting to be evangelised, had temporarily settled their differences and had written asking the Harms brothers to send missionaries to the region near Lake Eyre. Though Louis feared that Hermannsburg was overextending its capacity, he finally consented, provided that he remain the head of the enterprise and that in South Australia the missionaries account to a *Superintendent* (supervisor). The first of these requirements, which mirrored the hierarchical structure of the Lutheran Church, was clearly impractical because of the distance involved. The second was to lead to constant disagreement and quarrelling between the mission stations in the north and the church authorities in the south.

After their arrival in the Barossa, Gössling, Homann and Vogelsang lost little time in preparing for their journey inland. They tried to familiarise themselves with the peculiarities of the new continent and procured the ample provisions needed for the long and arduous trip. A fourth member, Ernst Jacob, who had emigrated to the Barossa from Silesia in the mid-1850s, joined the group as teamster. Finally, all preparations were complete and, amid lengthy ceremony and celebrations, the missionary expedition left Tanunda for the lake country of the Lower Cooper, east of Lake Eyre. The departure date (October) was not well chosen as they would soon face the forbidding summer heat. Their German wagons were not well suited for the desert tracks, and when one broke down the team was forced to abandon some of its luggage. They finally arrived at their destination and set up camp at Lake Killalpaninna, a flow-on from the Lower Cooper, on New Year's Eve 1866. Initially the Aborigines' reaction was friendly, which was not appreciated by the Christians:

> When we arrived the heathens offered their wives and daughters. We were shocked. How deep can a people sink if the guiding hand of the Lord does not provide protection against the ever-present seduction of the Devil. We grabbed our horse whips and lashed out at these wicked women, who made a hasty retreat.[8]

The missionaries' action did not endear them to the local Aborigines, who had already become extremely wary of their dealings with Europeans. And the desert climate took its toll immediately. All four men complained of eye sickness, and Gössling needed medical attention for sunstroke. Facing further hostilities from Aboriginal tribes, the Lutherans left the area in May – their first attempt at missionising having lasted less than five months – and headed back to the Barossa.

Their second attempt at Lake Killalpaninna was more enduring. They built a small settlement, which they called Neu-Hermannsburg and which included a school and a small church. They managed to establish more cordial relations with the Aborigines. A new assistant, Wilhelm Koch, quickly realised that previous descriptions of the Aborigines were crude and untrue. He found their language to be rich and beautiful, and he began to translate the New Testament into the local Dieri language. But hopes that their attempts at missionising were gaining momentum were soon dashed.

To begin with, the water level of the lake was falling. Less than a year after their arrival the missionaries wrote about what they regarded as an unusually pronounced drought, and throughout 1869 their letters expressed profound worries about the rapid drying out of Lake Killalpaninna and surrounding lakes. New sources of food and fresh water had to be found. Their initial attempts at digging wells met with little success, and there was a real threat that they would have to abandon the enterprise again. Drought conditions and desert heat continued to tax the physical and mental strength of the missionary colony, and lack of proper nourishment added to the perpetual problems of eye sickness and headaches.

Illnesses that under normal circumstances would have been cured by proper medical attention now proved fatal. Koch was the first victim. In 1869 he contracted typhus (the missionaries believed it was 'caused through the perspiration of the natives') and died soon after. The death toll continued. The colonist Vogelsang's wife, Dorothea, lost her first two children at birth, and although there may not have been a direct link between the babies' deaths and the desert conditions, the missionaries felt that their remoteness from medical care played a part in these tragedies.

Nor was progress with their church work as promising as they had earlier believed. The missionaries soon noticed a correlation between the food situation and the number of Aborigines visiting the station. When there was plenty of food and other supplies, the number of visitors was large, schools and church services were well attended and the enterprise seemed to be flourishing. But if resources ran low or good rains increased traditional food, numbers soon dwindled. Then there was the problem of teaching Christian values when the local Aboriginal language made little allowance for abstract spiritual or metaphysical terms. 'How can I teach them the happy message of the gospel', wrote Homann in frustration, 'when we can't translate such terms as mercy, sin, justice, sanctimony'. They tried to tell their pupils about the meaning of sin and the Devil 'but the young boys don't seem to be scared by the concept of hell, as to them it is a nice warm place'. It was this inability to get their message across 'which hurt more than all the other difficulties, the heat, the desert, the complete remoteness from all civilisation, the lack of resources'.[9]

Threatening confrontations with the Aborigines continued. The death of a young tribesman around Easter 1871 led to a large-scale *pindari* (blood-revenge) extending over several days. The Lutherans were caught in the middle when several men, fearing the deadly punishing parties, sought refuge at the mission station. The sudden appearance of troopers prevented major bloodshed. Not surprisingly, given these harsh conditions, the Europeans also quarrelled among themselves. 'The colonists made a lot of trouble for the missionaries', wrote Louise Homann; 'They wanted to be in charge of their own section of the mission and also of that of the missionaries.' This was also the case in Africa, where Mr Koch had often cried out in despair, 'we will never be successful here if there is disharmony'. But above all it was the lack of water that threatened the enterprise again. Some rain early in 1870 brought temporary relief, but by 1871 the lack of a reliable water supply was more worrying than before. Attempts to solve the problem by sinking more wells ended in disappointment.

The Homanns were the first to give up. In the spring of 1871, shortly after the birth of their third child, Louise Homann went south. The two sons of her first marriage had decided to further their education in Germany, and she had to arrange for their departure. She did not return. Her husband followed six months later and informed the mission committee in Tanunda that the situation at Lake Killalpaninna had become hopeless. Quarrels with the committee about further attempts to sink wells finally resulted in Homann's resignation at the beginning of 1872.

Hermannsburg sent out a new missionary, Carl Schoknecht, who arrived in the summer, just as the station was about to be abandoned. The last of the water had dried up, and the remaining settlers were forced to seek hospitality at the Mandowodana (also spelled Mundowdana) station near Herrgott Springs (now Marree). Schoknecht stayed here for almost two years, supervising further attempts to dig for permanent water supply (all failures) before giving up. A genuine 'new chum' to desert conditions, he was even less likely than Homann to continue the missionary enterprise. A year later Dorothea Vogelsang fell seriously ill. In a desperate attempt to save her life the couple rushed for medical attention south to Herrgott Springs, taking their son (her third birth had been successful) with them. Two days later she died in the arms of her husband.

It now seemed certain that Hermannsburg's first enterprise to Christianise Aboriginal people in Australia would not survive. The missionaries had given up, and the fragile compromise between the Lutheran churches in South Australia had collapsed. Traditional doctrinal issues again became the occasion for dispute, and it was decided that the Immanuel Synod of Australia should take over the mission station at Lake Killalpaninna, while the Evangelical-Lutheran Synod of Australia (ELSA) would set up a new mission station. And while strong voices among the church elders urged that Killalpaninna should be closed altogether, hopes were high that the new enterprise would be more successful. Again, missionaries and *Kolonisten* were sent out from Hermannsburg.

New Hermannsburg at the Finke

The history of the ELSA-sponsored enterprise dates from 22 October 1875, when a party of 8 men, 33 horses, 17 cattle and 3100 sheep set out from Bethany for the Finke River south of the Macdonnell Ranges. George Heidenreich, pastor at Bethany parish, was given the position of *Superintendent* of the new station and was put in charge of the expedition. The two missionaries were Hermann Kempe and Wilhelm Schwarz. Kempe had previously been a blacksmith, and Schwarz a baker. Theodor Harms is said to have joked that he chose them for mission work in Central Australia because they were already accustomed to heat. The other members were colonists and assistants for the journey. Heidenreich felt optimistic; he hoped to lead the party to its destination and be back in time for Christmas. He miscalculated by seventeen months.

The team was immediately affected by a massive drought. It took them six months to reach Stuart's Hole on the Neales River. Driven by their strong faith in God, all survived, although they were in a state of complete physical and spiritual exhaustion. Almost 1000 sheep and several horses and bullocks perished. At last it rained, and on 29 May they reached the unfailing Dalhousie Springs. Drought conditions further north forced most of the party to set up camp there for almost a full year. A small, highly equipped expedition did strike ahead and reached the country of the Finke River, where a beautiful view of the river and the surrounding Macdonnell Ranges filled the men with great delight. They returned to Dalhousie Springs and holed up until April 1876. Not until 7 June 1877 were they finally able to select their site, which they, like the first team ten years previously, called Hermannsburg.[10]

Over the next two years one more missionary, Louis Schulze, joined the station, accompanied by more colonists, and a little later a number of brides arrived. By 1880 all missionaries and some of the colonists were married, and offspring soon followed. They built a sizeable settlement consisting of several neatly planned houses. The missionaries' initial plans to pursue agriculture rather than pastoralism were not realised, although they conducted some ingenious experiments, not all of which were immediate failures. However, the livestock flourished and soon brought good returns; in fact, revenue from livestock made the station virtually self-sufficient. A decade or so after their arrival all seemed well, but for the greatest problem most missionaries faced: how to convert 'Godless heathens' into God-fearing Christians.

Kempe, Schwarz and Schulz took a gradual approach. They were fortunate in that the local tribe, the Arrernte (then spelled Aranda), were less aggressive than the Dieri had been. Perhaps one reason for this was that the Arrernte had not come into contact with Europeans prior to the Lutherans' arrival and were still ignorant of the implications. Encounters with the Arrernte were few during the first years. As with Lutheran missionaries elsewhere, the pastors at Hermannsburg intended to attract the Aborigines to the station, persuade them to give up their 'nomadic' existence and settle at the mission. They then hoped to convert them to the Lutheran faith and so ensure the eternal welfare of their souls. In order to achieve this, the missionaries planned to place the station on a sound economic basis and establish local industries offering regular employment. Once the Aborigines had settled at the mission under the care of the Christians, and had adopted a white lifestyle, a full conversion to Christianity could be made. However, as the earlier Lutheran missionaries had discovered, there was a direct correlation between climatic conditions and mission attendance: when there was a drought and a shortage of food, church and mission school attendance was high; but come the rain and an abundance of animals, plants and birds, few Arrernte were to be seen.

For the first ten years the missionaries stuck at their task and took heart from any progress, however modest. In 1887 a small group of seven Aborigines were baptised, which provided a ray of hope. There were even signs that the missionaries had begun to understand the culture and life of the Arrernte. Yet in the end the Hermannsburg missionaries at the Finke River were also defeated, not necessarily because of their own inability but because of the policies pursued by their superiors in the south. The missionaries' requests for periods of recreation away from their exhausting life in Central Australia were constantly refused and, as a result of doctrinal quarrels, the church fathers finally lost interest in the enterprise altogether. The German chronicler sums up a disastrous failure:

> If we look at the Hermannsburg enterprise in Australia we have to say: it was a painful tragedy. Started with hopes and big expectations, carried out under enormous strains and great costs which seemed to have been justified by promising expectations, our connection here brought one bitter disappointment after the other and failed not because of the stubbornness of hard-hearted heathens but because of petty doctrinal quarrelling.[11]

Religious differences were one reason for their lost labour, and physical exhaustion the other. For years, Kempe informed Harms that the climate was robbing them of their strength. The summers brought regular bouts of dysentery and inflamed eyes and the winters brought viral and pulmonary infections. In 1888–89 a severe outbreak of influenza was followed by a typhoid epidemic. Schwarz was the first to give up. He left for the south in 1889, physically debilitated and spiritually exhausted. Moreover, the continuous deterioration in the Aborigines' living conditions sapped the missionaries' morale. By the late-1880s diseases, especially syphilis, were affecting virtually the whole Indigenous population. In addition, the missionaries feared that there were few ways to stop the white settlers from either shooting the Aborigines or intoxicating them, or having sexual relationships with Aboriginal women. They felt that all their attempts to avert the threatening genocide were useless. One colonist after another was forced to leave. Schulze carried on until October 1891, when he became so weak that Kempe insisted on his departure. A few weeks later Kempe's wife, the mother of five children, died along with one of her sons. In November the last of the missionaries reluctantly left the station. He was so weak that he had to be lifted onto the wagon that carried him and his surviving children south.

A few colonists carried on for another year, after which Hermannsburg lay empty until a new team from the south rode into the station one hot day in October 1894:

> [There] were no hymns or gay Christian voices, only the vacant stare of two aged and naked heathen Aranda lounging on loose sand. The sharp outline of buildings and the greenery of palm trees alone reminded them of the labours of the Hermannsburg missionaries; and the walls of the church and the school were slowly tumbling to earth.[12]

The new missionary, Carl Strehlow, knew that he had a long and difficult job ahead.

The Neuendettelsauer Missionsanstalt

Despite all the prognostications and the considerable reluctance of the church authorities to carry on, Lake Killalpaninna mission station had survived the first attempts to close it down. This was in part due to the tenacity of its colonists, especially the station's seniors, Hermann Vogelsang and Ernst Jacob, who showed little inclination to abandon the enterprise. Whether this was because of their strong religious convictions (as sometimes alleged) or because they had no prospects of comfortable positions as parish pastors and were reluctant to leave the station, is open to debate. Certainly the lay personnel strongly (and successfully) protested against the mission's closure. Their case was strengthened after the church elders, who were in favour of continuing, were able to reach agreement with the Neuendettelsauer Missionsanstalt near Nuremberg in Franconia, which began to send out missionaries in 1878.

The Neuendettelsau missionaries and their helpers fared better. They built on the foundations laid by their predecessors. At the first 'Neu-Hermannsburg', which they renamed Bethesda, they were also fortunate in having a lengthy spell of favourable weather (the lower Cooper flooded several times during the 1880s); and the fact that the railway line was coming closer (it reached Farina in 1882 and Herrgott Springs in 1884) helped to reduce previous difficulties. In addition, it seems that the brothers Harms had been too restrictive in giving preference to young men of peasant/artisan background when selecting missionary trainees. There is, of course, no reason why smithies and bakers should not make good missionaries, but their approach greatly restricted the intake pool.

There is an air of greater competence around the Neuendettelsau enterprises. The first missionary, Johannes Flierl – referred to in mission circles as Flierl-Auricht – showed great stamina in establishing and running mission stations, although he was almost completely impervious to the culture and lifestyle of the people he attempted to missionise. He turned Bethesda into a flourishing settlement comprising a dozen buildings and an impressive church, and he baptised the first heathens. But when news came that the German Empire had annexed the southeastern part of New Guinea, he applied for a transfer to the new colony, which was far more densely populated than

Australia and hence offered a more promising field to the missionary. He later recalled:

> The thought of going to New Guinea as the pioneer missionary took a strong hold upon me and I had to do what I could in the matter. I sat down and wrote in detail what was on my mind, that we German Lutherans in Australia ought to begin this mission work, and why we ought to do it.[13]

After some hesitation by the authorities in Germany and the Barossa, Flierl's request was granted and he left for New Guinea. Others were sent to continue the work in Australia.

Over the next ten years, three of the young men sent out from Neuendettelsau proved to be talented missionaries who all left their mark. They were Johannes Reuther, who ran the Bethesda station from 1888 to 1906; Carl Strehlow, who began his work as missionary at Bethesda in 1892, before he took over the abandoned second Hermannsburg station at the Finke River in 1894; and Otto Siebert, who worked at Bethesda between 1893 and 1902. These missionaries gained a good understanding of the Aborigines' traditional life and began to grasp the full richness of Aboriginal culture. Reuther, ranked by a historian of the Lutheran Church as the most outstanding missionary to work among the Dieri,[14] collected a large number of Aboriginal sculptures and artefacts. However, he left the station under controversial circumstances in 1906 when involvement with a black girl was alleged. Although there seems to have been no justification for this claim, the authorities accepted the validity of the rumour, which illustrates the difficulties inherent in a hierarchical set-up that subordinated the mission to people far removed from the scene.[15]

Between 1893 and 1902 Reuther was assisted by Siebert, who immediately showed keen interest in the Dieri people. Siebert was to spend a great deal of his time away from the mission, living with tribal groups on the outskirts of the station, where he gained an understanding of Aboriginal life and culture second to none. In fact, it is likely that Siebert's decision to return to Germany was due not to declining health but to doubts about the purpose of his works. He began to feel that it was wrong to attempt to change the lifestyle of the Aboriginal people.[16]

Regrettably, the last missionary at Bethesda, Wolfgang Riegel, who arrived in 1908 (two years after Reuther had left), was not able to match his predecessor's ability. For him to have been sent to Australia – in *Zögling* circles a dead-end assignment, as it was widely believed that the Aborigines were a dying race – was a great disappointment. He had hoped to be sent to New Guinea, which was held to offer a flourishing future. The station at Lake Killalpaninna confirmed his worst expectations. It was run down and there was little sign that progress had been made in converting the Aborigines, whose numbers were dwindling year by year.

Inexperienced, he attempted to introduce measures that bore no relation to the Aborigines' lifestyle. Constant quarrelling with the church authorities did not help his spirits and, completely disillusioned, he gave up after four years. His departure in 1912 marked the effective end of the Bethesda mission station. Hermann Vogelsang's eldest son (also called Hermann) continued to run the school for a short while, but it was closed during World War I in the wake of the anti-German feelings that prevailed in South Australia. The remnants of the Dieri tribes dispersed into the vast interior. None of those tribes has survived.

After a short spell at Bethesda, Carl Strehlow took over the second Hermannsburg in 1894 and ran it in competent fashion until his death in 1922. He managed to win the confidence of the Arrernte and neighbouring tribes and his close relationships enabling him to pursue valuable anthropological and ethnological studies, which he published in seven parts as *Die Aranda – und Loritja Stämme in Zentral Australien*. He died tragically on his way south to seek medical attention. Although his anthropological work was outstanding, his name fell into oblivion after his death, partly because of the postwar anti-Germanism and partly because his work was at odds with the dominant anthropological establishment of the time. His reputation, however, has recently been restored.[17]

Missionary work at Hermannsburg was continued by Karl Albert who, like Strehlow, assisted the Aborigines in their fight for survival. Both men and their helpers can claim some credit for the fact that the people of the Arrernte tribes did not share the fate of the Dieri – and in 1982, control of the Hermannsburg settlement was handed back to them.

There was one more German-run mission station that managed to survive until placed under Aboriginal administration in the 1980s. This was the Catholic Beagle Bay station, 160 kilometres north of Broome, where German Pallottine monks had worked among the local Njul Njul tribe for almost a century. Missionary activities had ceased much earlier at the Moravian Brothers' Weipa station on the west coast of Cape York Peninsula and at the Lutheran station at the Bloomfield

River south of Cooktown, but these stations did survive as Aboriginal settlements.

The chequered history of the Lake Killalpaninna and Finke River mission stations illustrates the difficulty of making generalisations about the work of the missionaries. Too often they are dismissed as incompetent, blinded by their religious faith, and failing to understand the life and culture of Indigenous people. In terms of the number of Aborigines converted, the results were modest, and we might wonder whether they justify the sacrifices. People close to the missionaries and their calling, or with strong Christian beliefs, will no doubt argue so. Others have been more sceptical, but in my opinion, Mary Durack's conclusion to her study of the Beagle Bay mission is still very persuasive:

> [Those who see] progress in purely material terms may find little to have justified the continuance of these establishments in the face of such terrific odds. Those who seek evidence of the wholehearted conversion of the Aborigines and their satisfactory integration into the white man's social system may also find reason to doubt. Yet in a totally hostile world the missionaries, sometimes inspired, sometimes blind, provided the only evidence the Aborigines had of anything in the nature of consistent altruism within an otherwise ruthless and self-seeking economy. It provided a ray of hope in the prevailing gloom of their predicament. It was for many their only means of survival and their sole reason for regeneration.[18]

5

THE GOLDEN AGE

About 70 000 people from German-speaking countries migrated to Australia in the half-century between 1840 and 1890.[1] As it was common for German families to have many children, the number of people of German background might well have doubled by the beginning of the twentieth century. As it was, 5 or even 6 per cent of the total population was German-born or of German descent by 1890, with the majority living on the land or in small towns. For most, the decision to leave their *Heimat* and venture to a new life turned out to be a wise one. This nineteenth-century German immigration is largely a success story – for both the immigrants and the burgeoning new society. Some did not do so well and left the country, or died here, in disappointment – but their stories are few. Germans migrated to all six colonies, and South Australia led the way.

South Australia

The chain migration that followed the first wave of Old Lutherans from Prussia's central and eastern provinces continued unabated throughout the 1840s and into the 1850s. Half of the 7000 Germans who lived in South Australia in the early 1850s came from the Lutheran heartlands of Prussia. Partly subsidised by their own countrymen and partly by the Wakefield scheme, they had been rural dwellers in the old country and virtually all of them moved into the rural regions. Initially, the restrictive nature of the Wakefield system – which was based on the principle that land should be sold and not granted, so that the proceeds could be invested in further immigration – limited the room to move for most new arrivals. Land was dear, so potential farmers had to wait until their economic situation allowed the purchase of viable holdings. By 1850 there were two main areas of German settlement: to the east of Adelaide in the region around Mt Lofty, with Hahndorf at its centre, and to the north in the Barossa Valley. The Barossa, 40 kilometres long and 8 kilometres wide, was overwhelmingly German-speaking in its early years. Tanunda grew quickly into a busy township, and the numerous villages (Stockwell, Ebenezer, Rowland Flat, Greenoch, Lobethal, Nurioopta, Krondorf, to name some) were made up predominantly of settlers from German lands.

Initially, the villages were laid out in traditional farmlet form (*Hufendorf*), and as the new arrivals built their houses in the German timbered style (*Fachwerkhäuser*), places like Hahndorf, Paechtown and Bethany (the first settlement in the Barossa Valley) were unique in the Australian environment and soon became major tourist attractions.[2] However, with trees becoming scarce, bricks replaced timber, the *Hufendörfer* gave way to villages with streets (*Strassendörfer*), and the original thatched roofs were replaced by galvanised iron. The Germans proved to be reliable and industrious workers intent on acquiring their own property. Only a few fell victim to the 1850s gold fever that gripped so many in the colonies and overseas. Families allowed one son at most to try his luck in the goldfields while the rest of the family worked at the farm As one of them put it, 'We make gold with the plough'. And indeed they did. Germans took mainly to wheat farming, but took care not to become dependent on one crop, and so were able to keep their farms in times of crop failure or economic hardship.[3]

But not all German immigrants were farmers. Between 1845 and 1855, 1300 miners from the Claustahl-Zellerfeld area in the Harz mountains headed for the Burra coppermines in the north of the colony. Leadmining was no longer profitable in their home country so the Hanover government encouraged the emigration of unemployed miners by offering to advance their fares to Australia, to be repaid from their incomes in Burra. Louis Ballhausen, who became one of Victoria's leading mining entrepreneurs, was among those who accepted the offer. Together with his wife, mother and siblings he left for Adelaide in August 1849, keeping a detailed diary of the journey out. He worked in Burra for three years and then headed for the

An early immigrants' school in Langmeil, South Australia, around 1850 (Mortlock Library, State Library of South Australia)

Victorian goldfields, where he worked with modest success for the next fifteen months. Horse trading and the establishment of general stores in Launceston and Geelong were not much more profitable, but he struck it lucky with his attempt at wheat farming.

Ballhausen bought a property in the Barrabool Hills 15 kilometres west of Geelong and, having imported the most modern threshing machine, made a fortune. This enabled him to return in 1858 to Ballarat, where he purchased the Post Office Mine. The mine was believed to have seen its heyday but, with the aid of a 16-head quartz battery – the first in Ballarat – Ballhausen outwitted his competitors. He established several more mines in and around Ballarat, then for seven years took over the management of the famous Wentworth Company at Orange in New South Wales, before returning to Victoria to run mines in the region around Bright. Ballhausen retired in 1879 and returned to Ballarat, where he lived until his death in August 1908, his wife having passed away six weeks earlier. Their daughter and six sons all reached prominent positions in the eastern colonies and Western Australia.[4]

About 1000 Moravians from the Bohemian parts of the Habsburg Empire constituted another significant group of German-speaking immigrants to South Australia. And so did several hundred Wends, a Slavonic community who lived in Lusatia in southeastern Germany, either in the *Niederlausitz* (lower Lusatia), which was part of Prussia, or in the *Oberlausitz* (upper Lusatia), which belonged to Saxony. Having lived for centuries among Germans, the Wends (or Sorbs) were bilingual and generally regarded as Germans by the English-speaking population. Many participated in the movement of German farmers to Victoria in the 1850s (and later to New South Wales), where conditions regulating the acquisition of land were more favourable. All told, about 9000 Germans, or about 7 per cent of the population, had settled in South Australia by 1861.

New South Wales, Victoria and Tasmania

Large-scale German immigration to New South Wales and Victoria started, independently, in the late 1840s, and was above all the work of two capable and industrious entrepreneurs: Wilhelm Kirchner, a merchant in Sydney, and William Westgarth, a Melbourne businessman and politician. Kirchner was born in 1814, the fourth child of the Reverend Anton Karl Kirchner and his wife Sophia Frederika Dorothea. His father was a prominent burger of the city of Frankfurt. Well educated, he went to England at the age of eighteen and stayed with family friends in Manchester. Here he made the acquaintance of two Sydney merchants, Alec Campbell and Thomas Walker, who aroused his interest in Australia – an interest that was to shape his future. His business activities in Frankfurt and Manchester flourished over the next few years and in 1839 he had sufficient funds to book a cabin-class ticket to Sydney, where he set up a merchant firm. He continued to establish valuable business links and his residence became a meeting place for Sydney's small German community; Ludwig Leichhardt was among his visitors. Last – but certainly not least – he married in Sydney a local 'currency lass', Frances Murdoch Sterling.

By 1846 Kirchner began to submit to the colonial government, businessmen and pastoralists his suggestion for solving the colony's labour shortage: subsidised German immigration under a bounty scheme that granted a family an initial income of £20–25 per annum. He was appointed immigration agent for New South Wales in 1847, having become Consul for the City of Hamburg a year earlier, and left for Frankfurt with his family in February 1848. On the journey he drafted the manuscript for his *Australien und seine Vortheile für Auswanderer* (Australia and its advantages for emigrants), which proved an effective tool for attracting German migrants. There was no shortage of applicants and the first ship with 'bounty migrants', the *Beulah*, sailed from London on 10 December. Four more ships left from London in 1849, but as Kirchner had by now reached agreement with the Hamburg shipowner Johann Caesar Godeffroy, all subsequent emigration under his scheme left from Hamburg. The bulk of this first wave of migrants came from the southwestern states – Hesse, Baden and Württemberg – where times were particularly hard. By 1852 approximately 2000 Germans had disembarked in Sydney.[5]

Kirchner's idea to sign up whole families for assisted immigration paid dividends, as few of them fell victim to the gold fever. Instead, like the German families in South Australia, they were looking for rural life. Some went to the outskirts of Sydney, where they worked as vinedressers at the Macarthur properties around Camden or the Cox family vineyard at Penrith. On completion of their contracts they could afford to buy their own land at reasonable prices, for viticulture, orchards or market gardens. The same goes for numerous families who took up work in the Kiama/Shoalhaven region south of Wollongong. Still further south, the Kameruka Estate at Bega employed over twenty German families who acquired land in the district on completion of their contracts and who played an active part in the development of the South Coast dairy industry. But most popular for German settlers in the 1850s was the southwest: Albury, the Riverina and Germantown (today's Holbrook). To the northwest of Sydney, in Mudgee, Adam Roth – one of a number of vinedressers in this region – established the Rothview Estate, today's Craigmoor winery, still one of Australia's most famous wine producers. The Hunter Valley, too, boasted a large number of German pioneers, working in both wine-making and the pastoral industry – and so did the north coast. The country in and around Grafton and the adjacent Clarence River district accounted for further immigration during the 1850s, and Kirchner played a major part in the establishment of a German community by founding a soap and candle factory in Grafton in 1855.

In the Port Phillip District, records list eight Germans in 1842, living mainly in the Melbourne area. The family of Victoria's first governor, Charles La Trobe, was of Moravian background, and he himself had toured large parts of Germany as a young man. Interest in large-scale German immigration among Melbourne's leading circles dates back to the mid-1840s, when both rural areas and towns faced a severe shortage of labour. There were calls to bring in convicts from Van Diemen's Land, or even to ship them directly from Britain. In this context, the situation in neighbouring South Australia, where a steady stream of migrants from Germany was making a valuable contribution to the colony's prosperity, was keenly noticed. In early December 1846 an editorial in the *Port Phillip Gazette* had this to say:

> A healthy, useful, and moral emigration has been taking place during
> the last five years between Germany and South Australia. Our
> Adelaide contemporaries speak in the highest terms of their German
> Colonists – they are most industrious, temperate and peaceable in
> their habits; unexceptionable in their morals, and of sound religious
> principles. They have been accused of being narrow in their
> expenditure; but this is more than counterbalanced by the fact that
> they buy everything for ready money; in a word the thrifty German
> forms the *beau ideal* of a useful Colonist, and his industry is
> calculated to be of no ordinary advantage to the Colony he has
> selected for his future abode. We do not envy our neighbours their
> good fortune in possessing such a useful class of Colonists; but we
> think that, if possible, this District ought to take some steps to obtain
> a supply from the German Ports.[6]

William Westgarth, a leading Melbourne merchant who had arrived from Scotland in 1840, was the person chosen to take the matter further. Westgarth went to Europe in 1847 where, among other things, he explored the issue of bringing in German migrants under the newly established bounty system for non-British subjects. After negotiations that lasted for the best part of a year, he reached an agreement with a Bremen shipping agent, Eduard Delius, who had made a name for himself by recruiting German migrants for the South Australian Company.[7]

The first ship with German immigrants, the *Godeffroy*, left Hamburg on 1 October 1848. Three more followed, altogether bringing about 900 German migrants from north and northeastern Germany to the Port Phillip District by the end of 1849. The colonial bounty scheme stipulated that agricultural labourers be preferred, and in particular skilled vinedressers. But Delius turned out not to be as honest and reliable as Kirchner: on the four ships that arrived in 1849 there was scarcely a single vinedresser. Not surprisingly, the government was reluctant to pay the bounty. A large number of the new arrivals were of urban, predominantly lower-middle-class background, and since – according to the Melbourne newspapers – there were some 'dubious elements' among them, there were soon calls to stop assisted immigration from German-speaking countries

Westgarth managed to pacify the situation,[8] vinedressers soon arrived, and most of the Germans proved reliable and industrious migrants after all, settling chiefly in the Geelong and Melbourne districts. A few more ships brought more Germans in 1850 but, with Delius's resignation as agent that year, and the population explosion brought about by the discovery of gold a little later, German bounty migration to Victoria came to an end in 1851. Nevertheless, the gold rush of the 1850s meant that of the 30 000 or so Germans who came to Australia by 1861, over a third headed for Victoria.

The discovery of gold, coupled with the abolition of convict transportation in 1853, caused a serious labour shortage in Van Diemen's Land, which induced the colonial government there, too, to set up a bounty system. The government offered to pay all but £5 of the fare across. In return the immigrants had to contract to stay for at least four years in the colony.[9] Europeans were accepted and, in its encouragement of family emigration, the Tasmanian scheme was not unlike Kirchner's model. On the other hand, 'widowers and widows with young children, persons who intend to buy land, or to invest in Capital, or who are in the habitual receipt of parish relief, or who have not been vaccinated' were not encouraged to apply. Of the 5000 immigrants the offer attracted in 1855, 858 were Germans, chiefly from southwestern and northern Germany, who settled in and around Hobart and the Lilydale region.

In New South Wales the bounty scheme for migrants from Germany was suspended in 1857, although family-nominated immigration and private sponsorship continued. This cancellation was largely provoked by the appalling conditions on many of the ships. The three-month journey to Australia was always dangerous in the times before comfortable steam-liners. But during the peak years of continental migration unscrupulous agents and captains, keen to maximise their profits, tended to overcrowd their ships or failed to employ a competent crew (which had to include a ship's doctor), or neglected to carry adequate food and medical supplies. In the light of heavy death tolls on many of the journeys, the list of complaints made against German ships was very long.[10] The worst recorded case is that of the Hamburg-based *Caesar*, which left its home port in March 1855. Passengers were struck down by a succession of diseases, including cholera, which resulted in the deaths of 24 adults and 42 children – a fifth of those who had embarked. On the *Catteau Wattel*, which sailed to Australia at the same time, 3 adults and 22 children died. Evidence given to a New South Wales government inquiry in 1858 lists further harrowing stories. There were scores of complaints about the inadequate separate accommodation for men and women and the lack of proper medical care.

Wilhelm Kirchner was called upon as a witness, his business having already suffered from the cessation of assisted German immigration. More serious setbacks soon followed. The death of its chief candlemaker, Johann Martin Stelz, in December 1858 led to the demise of Kirchner's soap and candle factory at Grafton; Stelz had held a special patent and was not easily replaced.[11] Then in 1860 a small schooner that was transporting the family's furniture and other valuables for his new residence, Kirchnerstadt, was wrecked as it negotiated the entrance to the Clarence River near Yamba.[12] A year later his company was declared insolvent and he had to resign his position as consul. Yet Kirchner's skills as leading immigration agent for German migrants were soon to be called upon again, when in 1869 he was appointed immigration agent for Queensland. The newly founded colony was desperately short of people and again Germans were more than *willkommen*. Close to 6000 had settled there already.

Queensland

The generous Queensland Immigrant Regulations of 1860, which awarded a land order to the value of £18 per adult to the agent who subsidised their journey, quickly attracted entrepreneurs.[13] Johann Christian Heussler was appointed in March 1861 as Immigration Agent for Queensland on the Continent of Europe, and given charge of the lucrative German 'emigration market'. Born in 1820 at Bockenheim near Frankfurt into a Hessian merchant family, the keen business sense he showed from his early years eventually landed him in Victoria in 1852. His merchant enterprise did well in the gold districts of the colony, and he soon became acquainted with the immigration process – in fact he married William Westgarth's sister, Sophia Esther. As the weather in Victoria was detrimental to his health, the couple moved to the warmer climate of Brisbane in 1854. Here he ran a string of business activities, and in 1859 went into partnership with Reinhard Franksen, the Consul for the Duchy of Oldenburg from 1860 until his death in 1863. Franksen proved a reliable assistant to Heussler in his work as immigration agent. To entice people to Queensland he published *Kurze Beschreibung der Kolonie Queensland* (Short description of the colony of Queensland), which promised a land of milk and honey:

> Europeans will find in this colony a fine, salubrious climate suited to their constitution; a strong orderly government on the British model and good laws which guarantee the safety of property; regular communal institutions and civil order; full political and civil rights immediately upon naturalization; good schools for the education of their children; complete religious freedom for their families to worship in accordance with the dictates of conscience.[14]

Farmers and labourers were promised land grants on arrival, which allowed them 'to settle immediately on the agricultural reserves without having to make long distance journeys into the interior as was the case in North America'. The soil and mild climate permitted 'work the whole year around and to harvest 2 or 3 crops regularly'. All this ensured financial blessings for the 'thrifty and industrious'.

Many Germans responded. Most new arrivals, in contrast to New South Wales, came from Prussia's central and eastern provinces, although Heussler also attracted migrants from the southwest of Germany. However, he soon faced the twin problems of nineteenth-century immigration: unscrupulous profiteering by sub-agents and shipping companies. Payments to the agents and their sub-agents were made per capita. Given the lucrative offer by the Queensland government, sub-agents and their assistants tried to increase their income by any means at their disposal. One of their practices was to offer exaggerated promises of an easy 'get rich quick' life. At times the exaggerations were so blatant that German governments placed advertisements in newspapers warning potential emigrants to be careful, and informing them of the regulations covering migration to Queensland. Moreover, sub-agents often made very generous interpretation of the requirement that immigrants should be young and healthy, and there were soon complaints from the Queensland government that the quality of some left much to be desired. However, the migrants had their own complaints about the appalling conditions on the German ships taking them to Australia.[15]

Heussler's activities as official immigration agent soon became a source of complaint by German migrants, as they seemed to have overlapped with his private business affairs. As immigration agent, he arranged the shipping with the Godeffroy company, but as the shipper, he received the land orders for those immigrants who could not pay their own fare. A petition from German settlers to the Queensland

Johann Christian Heussler (John Oxley Library, State
Library of Queensland)

Legislative Assembly in July 1863 complained that Heussler was using his office 'more for his own benefit than the good of the Colony or the immigrants' and asked for a salaried agent who would be barred by contract from speculation or jobbery.[16] And, as in New South Wales, the appalling conditions on some of the German ships led to an official enquiry that questioned the desirability of assisted migration from Europe. When the Queensland government faced a serious financial crisis in the mid-1860s, subsidised German immigration to the colony was suspended in 1865.

This notwithstanding, Heussler must be credited with bringing several thousand new immigrants to Queensland,[17] the great majority of whom became reliable and successful settlers. Heussler continued to be a successful businessmen and politician, with twenty years' service as Consul for the German Empire and several years as a member of the Legislative Council.[18] German immigration was reintroduced in 1869, when Wilhelm Kirchner was made Agent-General for Queensland. A minority of these newcomers stayed in Brisbane, but most initially settled along the Logan River to the south. By the mid-1860s the first German had arrived in the inhospitable Rosewood scrub, and from here German immigrants spread into the Fassifern and the Lockyer Valley. The task they faced there was not an easy one.

Rural pioneers

In Queensland, migrants who had paid their own fare were immediately given land orders, which meant that many were able to 'select' an arable block of land soon after arrival. Those whose fares had been advanced had to wait until they had accumulated sufficient funds, which normally took no longer than two years. The size of allotments made available for selection ranged from 40 to 160 acres, and the price was fixed at £1 per acre.[19] A selector was required to pay the full amount in advance, but had to fulfil residence, fencing and cultivation requirements within twelve months before receiving the title. This meant hard work. As all the land was still virgin, the settlers had to begin by clearing a path to their selection for horse- or bullock-drawn carts, which carried not only the family's basic possessions but also sufficient food and supplies to last until a block had been cleared and vegetables harvested. Construction of shelter took priority and the first dwelling was normally a temporary hut made of mud and thatch, or slabs, and rarely with more than two rooms. Charles Meyer catches the spirit:

> Once settled, the whole family worked together to clear the scrub and to progressively establish a small general farm. We should not forget that in the 1860s and 1870s all agricultural work was done by hand – the felling of trees, the clearing of scrub and thick undergrowth, the grubbing of stumps, the ploughing of the virgin land and the sowing of seed. Even the initial watering was a manual job that could entail fetching water from sources miles away. It was only half jokingly that the Germans sometimes called Queensland 'Quälsland' (land of torment). The growing crops had to be protected from pests such as wallabies, rats and birds and this was usually a job for the children. Finally, the crops had to be hand-harvested and prepared for market. So there was precious little time in those years for cultural activities. On Sundays, families got dressed in their best clothes and ceased work to meet in the church, a powerful force for unity and

German settlers at the Taubi homestead in Tasmania

continuation of both German language and customs. Or, if there was
no church, families would meet at someone's house and conduct their
own service, using devotional books brought with them from their
homelands.[20]

And Ian Harmstorf highlights other basic shortcomings:

Sickness and accidents were common and every district had its
amateur dentist, equipped with a special hooked instrument, a bucket
to sit on, and no drugs to ease pain. There would also be a midwife,
usually an ordinary housewife, and a man capable of setting broken
bones, if only in a rough way. Every home had its box of patent
medicines, and home remedies such as cobwebs to stop bleeding
were common; but in cases of serious illness or accident the patient
often died from lack of skilled attention. The nearest doctor was
usually in the town, often a great distance from the farm. If the
person died, the grave was often under a tree in the bush, sometimes
roughly fenced off, sometimes not. Only where churches had been
built were there any graveyards, and although these were built very
soon after settlement, the Queensland scrub contains many a roughly
marked, nameless grave. This was a source of much distress for the
settlers, for whom Christian burial in hallowed ground was part of
demonstrated faith.[21]

Although the terms of land acquisition differed from colony to colony, the early pioneer work would have been the same everywhere. Both extracts show the great importance of the church in the settlers' lives. Construction of a church was undertaken as soon as the period of settling-in was over, and in these early days the pastor was often the schoolmaster. After a few years, subsistence farming would give way to specialised cash-crop production. Improvement in roads and the introduction of rail opened up new horizons; for many this meant a prosperity they could only have dreamed of in Germany. Not surprisingly, the German pioneers received a lot of praise. This much-cited comment was made to the parliament by the Queensland premier, Thomas McIlwraith, during a debate on immigration:

> The Germans arrive from the migrant ship in their German costumes; for one or two days they stay at the migrant hostel and then they suddenly disappear into the bush. Nothing more is heard of these people, until 18 months to two years later they suddenly reappear on the scene. And how? The man, his wife and children come driving into town in a wagon spanned to well groomed horses; are well dressed and on their faces one can see a certain contentment.[22]

This description is a touch rosy, but the Germans certainly did not shrink from hard work. Henry Lawson wrote that there were areas in New South Wales 'where no farming worthy of the name was possible – except by Germans and Chinamen'. And reports of inquiries into immigration held by the New South Wales government in 1870 contain flattering comments:

> The Germans are an excellent class of people; they are a good working people, and generally bring a small amount of money with them; they congregate together, are very sober and temperate in their habits; and are generally most useful labourers and good agriculturalists.

Another witness to the inquiry argued that the Germans were preferable to the Irish because they were 'of a high standard and desirable character – well educated, well trained men, and men of great industry'.[23] The *Cyclopedia of Victoria* speaks of districts in the colony where the land was held almost entirely by Germans 'whose superior frugality and simpler ways of life enabled them in many cases to buy out their British and Australian-born neighbours'.[24] A study of Boonah in Queensland maintains that the German immigrant generation 'succeeded in transforming some of the most forbidding tracts of wilderness into productive farmlands through sheer hard work'.[25]

The fact that so many Germans were pioneers in the bush raises the question of their relationships with the Indigenous people during the bloody confrontations that marked European settlement. References to contact with Aborigines are surprisingly few. Most comments are favourable, describing the Aborigines as friendly, helpful people who 'brought us fish, kangaroo tails, crabs or honey, to barter for our flour, sugar, tea, or "tumbacca"'. Nevertheless, some of the more outspoken tribe members are said to have questioned the white men's right to take over their land, and it was noticed that after white settlement the number of Aborigines declined rapidly. Of a tribe in the Logan district numbering 110 people in 1863, only 17 were left by 1887, with 'only two young gins . . . likely to keep up the stock'.[26]

Peak years

Between 1861 and 1890 the number of Germans settlers rose substantially. In some years as many as 2500 emigrants are listed as having left the ports of Bremen and Hamburg alone. On average, 1000 Germans emigrated to Australia per annum in this period. South Australia continued to receive a steady stream of Germans and, with the passing of the Strangeway Act in 1869 – modelled on the selection Acts of Queensland and Victoria, it offered larger areas of land on terms competitive with other colonies – German farmers soon moved into the mid-north of the colony, the Murray Flats and York Peninsula. The Strangeway Act also brought to a halt the movement of German migrants into the eastern colonies. Unhappy with the difficult conditions that until then had regulated the purchase of land, Germans and Sorbs had moved into the Hamilton region of Victoria in the early 1860s, and later in the decade into Victoria's Wimmera, and the Walla Walla township in New South Wales. In the late 1870s the Mallee, allegedly *the* most difficult country to pioneer, became another centre for German settlement in Victoria.

Disappointed gold-diggers added to the population in Victoria and New South Wales, which in 1891 listed 10 772 and 9565 German-born settlers respectively. Of the thousands of German diggers some did strike it rich,[27] but most had to look for a settled existence on the land or in the rapidly growing 'big smoke'. Next to English, German was the most common language spoken on the goldfields,[28] and a number of Germans were at the forefront of the Eureka Stockade. The

W. Burge's saddlery in Crows Nest, Queensland (John Oxley Library, State Library of Queensland)

gravestone at Ballarat's old cemetery lists three names: W. Emmermann from Hanover, J. Hafele from Württemberg and E. Thonen from Elberfeldt, referred to at the Ballarat Museum as the lemonade man. Frederick De Vern is reported to have ordered the other diggers in a loud voice: 'You – build barricades'.[29] This might account for the fact that he had the dubious honour of having the highest reward offered for his capture – and that he was lost sight of so quickly.

Queensland was the most popular choice for German immigration from the beginnings of the 1860s. The numbers eased temporarily when assisted German immigration was suspended in 1865, but the Queensland government soon had second thoughts and appointed the tireless Wilhelm Kirchner as the new immigration agent. Kirchner took up his new position with great energy, but bad luck continued to plague him when a first shipment of almost 1000 migrants was held up at Hamburg harbour because the outbreak of the Franco-Prussian War in July 1870 had led to a French blockade of German ports. By the time the war ended in the spring of 1871, the emigrants were destitute.

Once the war was over the situation improved a great deal, and 4000 new settlers came to Queensland over the next five years. Some of

Main Road in Marburg, Queensland, a century ago (John Oxley Library, State Library of Queensland)

them joined their countrymen in the Lockyer Valley and the Fassifern, but from the early 1870s onward they also moved into the Darling Downs and the South Burnett, with Toowoomba soon becoming the centre of German settlement in the colony. Approximately 400 families had settled there by 1890. In some parts of the Darling Downs there were German farmers with 1000 or more acres devoted to wheat and livestock, many of whom had come, with capital, from South Australia or Victoria. But the overwhelming majority ended up with small, intensively farmed holdings. In the Toowoomba district, for example, the German-owned farms mostly ranged from 5 to 40 acres, and grew fruit, vegetables and dairy produce.[30]

A number of Germans established settlements to the north of Brisbane, towards the Sunshine Coast, from the 1860s onwards. Subsequently, Germans from the south and those arriving directly from the mother country began to settle in central and northern Queensland, from Maryborough to Rockhampton. There they made an important contribution to the development of the sugar industry, principally as cultivators of cane for the central mills. By 1890 about 200 Germans, mainly from Pomerania, derived a livelihood from sugar-cane cultivation in the Bundaberg district. Another 100 or so were engaged in the same activity in the Mackay district, where a Lutheran church was erected in 1879. In isolated northwest Queensland, the discovery of gold at Charters Towers in 1872 attracted a number of Germans, of whom some 250 remained by the end of the century. The latter included a few who, like Heinrich Paradies and Friedrich Pfeiffer, struck it extremely rich indeed.

As the era of passenger sailing vessels entered its final years, the familiar problem of complaints about poor on-board conditions resurfaced, and in 1874 Kirchner's contract was cancelled again. Five years later, the Queensland government accepted the offer of the Hamburg shipowners H. C. Sloman and Co. to introduce steamships for the Australia run. This not only cut the travelling time by more than half, but their increased size meant that overcrowding and unsanitary conditions were soon a thing of the past. Compared to their predecessors, immigrants in the 1880s travelled in almost luxurious conditions.

In Tasmania, the original German immigrants of the mid-1850s, who had established settlements in Falmouth, St Mary's, Heidelberg, Leipzic, Collins Vale (originally Bismarck) and in particular Lilydale (originally German Town, later Upper Piper), were joined by a further 450 countrymen in the 1870s and 1880s. They came under a bounty system introduced by the Tasmanian government in 1870 that was modelled upon the Queensland system. They appointed Frederick Buck, a German who had arrived with the first wave of immigrants in the mid-1850s, to act as agent for Germany and Denmark. Like Delius, Kirchner and Heussler, Buck painted a glorious picture of life in the new land. Germans now accounted for the largest group of non-British settlers in Australia.

Only in Western Australia were immigrants from central Europe outnumbered, by Chinese and Malays. A sprinkle of German families had settled in the Swan River colony throughout the nineteenth century but here, too, it was not until the discovery of gold that the population began to rise dramatically (from 50 000 in 1891 to 185 000 in 1901), and with it the number of Germans (from 290 to 1522). The first major group to arrive, in the second half of the 1880s, were farmers from South Australia who took up properties in the wheat-belt district around the town of Katanning. As in the eastern colonies, many newcomers tried their luck at the goldfields, and sooner or later either returned to their homeland or settled for a more reliable livelihood. The large number of German businesses and

Berlin House, Hill End, New South Wales (Holtermann Collection, Mitchell Library, State Library of New South Wales)

other enterprises in and around Fremantle and Perth illustrates that the German diggers in Western Australia also followed this practice.[31]

As a recent study aptly puts it, 'the German settler was one of the most highly prized of all immigrants to Australia. As they were an Aryan [sic] kinfolk, possessing similar cultural traditions and speaking a related language, Australia could hardly get enough of them'.[32]

Urban dwellers

Whereas German communities in the countryside were relatively homogeneous, settlers in the cities were much more varied. Most were artisans and skilled workers. In the early mass-migration years, they worked mainly in the retail sector, in service industries and in skilled trades such as printing, cabinet-making and tailoring. Given the rural background of many of them, the acquisition of a small freehold block of land was one of their first priorities. Germans were also well represented in the small-business community, as shopkeepers and salesmen, and in the entrepreneurial class: many import, merchant and manufacturing firms were in German hands. They abounded among musicians, architects and artists, and many second- and third-generation Germans were teachers – from primary to tertiary level. They were over-represented in the natural sciences but under-represented among lawyers and doctors. With the exception of South Australia and to a lesser degree Queensland, few held political office at upper levels, though they were active in local politics everywhere.

Whereas the rural settlements remained firm bastions of political conservatism in all the colonies, urban Germans made a significant contribution to the development of liberalism (in the European sense) in Australia. This dates back to the middle of the nineteenth century, when a small but influential group of '48ers' – people who had fled the continent to escape political persecution and imprisonment after the aborted revolution of 1848. Most of them arrived in Adelaide in August 1849 on the *Princess Louise*, and probably the most well known were brothers Otto and Richard Schomburgk, and Carl Wilhelm Ludwig Muecke.

Muecke, the son of a teacher, was born in 1815 in Prussia's Magdeburg country. He followed his father's profession but, because of the radical views on education and politics he published in articles for the *Pädagogische Jahrbücher*, he soon ran into trouble with the Prussian authorities. His participation in the 1848 revolution further eroded his position as teacher and educator, and the imminent failure of the revolution led him to depart for Australia with his wife and three children. In 1850, together with Otto Schomburgk, he founded the *Südaustralische Zeitung*, and he played an influential part in the German press for the next four decades. He was also a Lutheran pastor to many congregations for almost twenty years, although it is said that his liberal views were watched with considerable suspicion by the Old Lutherans in the Barossa. Throughout his life he lectured and published on politics and education. By the time of his death in January 1898 he had become one of the most respected and well-known members of South Australia's cultural scene.

The same could be said of the brothers Otto and Richard Schomburgk, originally from Saxony. Otto Schomburgk, like Muecke, was involved in the local German press for the rest of his life. He also worked as a medical practitioner, ran a veterinary clinic and had a sound reputation as an architect. Furthermore, he was a Justice of the Peace and preached at the Lutheran church at Buchenfelde near Gawler. In addition to all this, he assisted his brother Richard on his property, Richard being among the German founders of the Barossa Valley wine industry. From 1861 to 1890 Richard held the directorship of the Adelaide Botanic Garden. He had learned his trade in the parks and gardens of Sans Souci, the famous residence of Frederick the Great. Like von Mueller in Melbourne, he published extensively, was a member of numerous societies around the world, and had received many honours and awards by the time of his death in March 1891.

Another '48er' (though not a passenger on the *Princess Louise*) who made a name for himself in South Australia was Eduard Heinrich Wulf Krichauff. He was elected to the first colonial parliament as member for Mount Barker in 1857, with the express purpose of passing the Real Property Act. Although this Act became known as the Torrens Title, after Sir Robert Torrens, the idea of a simple transfer of documents originated in the Hanseatic cities and the South Australian model was drafted by Ulrich Hübbe, Torrens's chief adviser. Hübbe was awarded a parliamentary pension for his services.[33] Having achieved his aim, Krichauff retired from the Legislative Assembly soon afterwards. The 28 mile walk from his farm near Strathalbyn probably clinched his decision. He returned to parliament twice: holding the seat of Victoria from 1870 to 1882, and of Onkaparinga from 1884 to 1890. He was a member of the Central Agricultural Bureau and the council of Roseworthy Agricultural College, became a strong advocate of reforestation schemes, and wrote numerous articles on such subjects as artesian water, beet sugar, and the use of fertilisers in field and garden.

Melbourne, too, received its share of '48ers'. There was Carl Ludwig Becker, political radical, poet, artist and scientist. Another political man of letters was Hermann Püttmann. Influenced in his early youth by the German Enlightenment, by the time he was forced to flee Germany he had a reputation for radical revolutionary writings. In Australia he enjoyed a long and successful career as writer and journalist. Püttmann was the publisher or co-publisher of several German-language weekly and monthly periodicals, and his many books ranged from a study of the tragic fate of the Burke and Wills expedition to a German songbook for Australia. In his political writings Püttmann was critical of the conservatism of British institutions, although he recognised that they safeguarded a political and religious freedom that in Australia might lead to a genuinely democratic society.

Adolf Heinrich Friedrich Bartels was one of Adelaide's most successful businessmen. Aged thirty, he arrived in the revolutionary year 1848, but it was entrepreneurial spirit and not politics that brought him to Australia. The son of a prosperous German merchant family, he had inherited a large fortune when his young wife, Josephine Olivia, whom he married in 1844, died shortly after childbirth in 1846. Bartels first accepted an arrangement with Joseph Ernst Seppelt, who required assistance and financial aid to establish his wine-growing business. In 1852 Bartels visited Ballarat and had a brief shot at digging for gold, before establishing an agency for fodder, grain and mining implements to provide a more reliable income. The first branch was in Ballarat, but his business chain soon extended to Melbourne and Geelong. Trade was so good that he expanded his agency by importing a full range of goods, especially furniture from Germany and the United States. Later he set up headquarters in Adelaide, where he became the director of several trading companies including the Permanent and Equitable Building Society, which financed the construction of many Adelaide houses. Thus he must rank as one of the most successful businessmen in Adelaide's early history. He was the lord mayor of that city between 1871 and 1873, and died rich and respected in 1878.

Hugo Carl Emil Muecke, son of the famous '48er', Carl Wilhelm, was just as successful with his enterprises. His company, H. Muecke and Co. was the largest Adelaide customs and shipping firm; it owned large bond stores at Port Adelaide, handled consignment and customs businesses, acted as agent for numerous freight and passenger lines, and owned and operated small coastal vessels. Between 1882 and 1914 he was Consul for Germany. His long list of offices includes the presidency of the Adelaide Chamber of Commerce, the directorship of BHP, and board membership of the Bank of Adelaide and the Executor Trustee & Agency Company of South Australia.

Johannes Nepomuk Detogardi, of Graz in Austria, arrived in Sydney with his wife in 1853 when he was thirty years old, and established a successful printing, publishing and photographic business. He edited the first German-language newspaper in Sydney, published a highly acclaimed book about the art of printing, and was among the first photographers in Sydney.

Fame as a photographer was also won by Johannes Wilhelm Lindt, born in 1845 in Frankfurt. He had been hired as a seaman and came to Australia after deserting a Dutch sailing ship in Brisbane, but soon became interested in the newly developing art of photography. He set up a business in Collins Street in Melbourne in 1876 and his society, theatre and landscape photographs enjoyed great popularity. By the 1880s he had achieved international acclaim, receiving prizes and medals at photographic exhibitions in London, Amsterdam, Frankfurt and Calcutta. He retired to a quiet but magnificent mansion that he

A Lindt photograph of shipboard life in the late 1880s; the men play cards while the women mind the children (State Library of Victoria)

built near the Black Spur beyond Healesville, and he died at the age of eighty-one during the 1926 Victorian bushfire disaster.

Theodor Karl – known as Charles – Troedel was one of Melbourne's finest lithographers. Aged twenty-four, Troedel arrived in Melbourne in 1860 and over the next thirty years set up flourishing lithographic businesses there and in Sydney. Also in Melbourne, Octavius Beale and Hugo Wertheim did well for themselves, producing high quality, expensive pianos; and in Sydney John Korff, son of a Brunswick family, set up a flourishing shipping business. Johann Menz in Adelaide established a successful biscuit and chocolate factory, and Germans were found among piano, and cigar and cigarette manufacturers.[34] Josef Kronheimer, for example, was the director of the W. D and H. O. Wills company before the Great War.

Some Germans did very well indeed at the goldmines, enabling them to settle into prosperous urban life. Friedrich August Pfeiffer was born in Worms in the Palatinate on 25 October 1844. He migrated to Australia at the age of twenty-one, and was successful from the start. With a number of his countrymen he established the Day-Dawn

Bernard Otto Holtermann (Mitchell Library, State Library of New South Wales)

goldmine near Charters Towers, which netted them several million pounds, and he invested in other profitable mining enterprises in the area. He became one of Charters Towers's leading citizens, and it is said that despite his wealth – he left an estate of around £300 000 – he remained a straightforward, modest and decent fellow. He certainly always retained a soft spot for Germany and the German people. There was a flourishing German community in Charters Towers and Pfeiffer supported their enterprise by building an impressive clubhouse, a German school and a spectacular church that was far more stately than the Lutheran churches in the capital cities. This evangelical community, made up of Germans from Pomerania, Silesia, Brandenburg and Württemberg, was until the twentieth century the only Australian congregation to be affiliated with the Prussian Evangelical church. Pfeiffer died, aged seventy, in Charters Towers.

A Holtermann photograph: Holtermann's Residence at St Leonard's, New South Wales (Mitchell Library, State Library of New South Wales)

Bernard Otto Holtermann, born in Hamburg in 1838, also emigrated in his youth. He tried his luck on and off the goldfields around Bathurst for the best part of twelve years. Fortune came his way in October 1871 when he discovered the world's largest specimen of reef gold, weighing nearly 300 kilograms. He did not squander his sudden wealth, but invested his money wisely. He became a foundation member of the Hill End Borough Council and built a magnificent house for his family at St Leonards, overlooking Sydney. He then devoted all his time to his great passion – photography – and won international fame during the 1870s and 1880s with his pictures of the goldfields and the countryside, and especially the magnificent panoramic shots of Sydney, for which he was commissioned. Today his photographs provide us with an excellent record of life in Sydney at that time. In 1882 Holtermann became the local member for St Leonards in the Legislative Assembly, but he died suddenly and prematurely in 1885, on his forty-seventh birthday.

A Holtermann photograph: Mining at Hill End (Mitchell Library, State Library of New South Wales)

Carl (later anglicised to Charles) Rasp, one of the co-founders of the Broken Hill Proprietary Company, also tried his luck first on the goldfields, before making his fortune in silver and lead mining. Rasp, according to historian Geoffrey Blainey, was 'a lean German with a small balding head and squirrel eyes' who grew up in Stuttgart in the Kingdom of Württemberg. He later moved to northern Germany, where he worked as a chemist in edible oils in Hamburg. In 1868, after a particularly severe winter, he decided to emigrate to Australia because a weakness in his lungs made him long for a warmer climate. He arrived in Melbourne in 1869 and headed immediately for the goldfields. However, he had no luck and the humidity of the shafts gave him a hacking cough – so he became a drover for Walwa Station on the Upper Murray and then a boundary rider in far-western New South Wales, where he was known as German Charlie. Often passing close to Broken Hill, he became so intrigued by the heavy black mineralised outcrops that he took out a mining lease with two partners. Success

A Holtermann photograph: McMahons Point, North Sydney, looking towards Sydney (Mitchell Library, State Library of New South Wales)

came only after they were joined by four more associates, who invested £70 each. In 1885 they discovered rich silver ore, and five years later Rasp had made a fortune. Although connected to Broken Hill mining for many years, he moved to Adelaide in 1886 and married Agnes Klevesahl. The couple were known for their lavish lifestyle and entertaining. Rasp, like Holtermann, died suddenly from a heart attack, on 22 May 1907.

There were, of course, ways to become rich other than by finding gold (or silver). Wilhelm Carl Vahland gained wealth through his architectural skills. He was born in 1828 in the Kingdom of Hanover and trained as an architect in several technical institutions. He arrived in Melbourne in 1854 and after a short stay went to Bendigo, which had succeeded Ballarat as the centre of goldmining in Australia. Here his services were much sought after. Among the many fine buildings that Vahland designed, partly in company with countryman Robert Elogius Hermann Getzschmann, are the Town Hall, the School of Mining, the Mechanics' Institute, the Masonic Hall and the Benevolent Asylum, as well as numerous splendid residences for Bendigo's mining magnates. The two architects were part of a small but prominent group of Germans in Bendigo, including Otto Waschatz, an artist who lectured in the School of Mines and did most of the interior decoration for the main hall of the Town Hall, and Herr Gollmiek, a composer and conductor of the Bendigo Philharmonic Orchestra.

Architects, more than any other professionals, put their stamp on the silhouettes of cities and towns. Among them was Frederick Bernhardt Menkens, born the son of a master mason in 1854 in Varel, a small town near Oldenburg in northwestern Germany. He had a sound apprenticeship in architecture, but the constant threat of unemployment prompted him to emigrate and he arrived, aged twenty-two, in Adelaide in November 1876. For six years he tried his luck in towns and cities throughout southeastern Australia until he finally settled in Newcastle. He established a most successful architectural firm and greatly contributed to the development of that city by designing over one hundred buildings, including St Andrews Cathedral, the Baptist Tabernacle, the Earp Gilliam Bond Store, Wood's Chambers and the School of Arts. He retired in 1908, moved to Sydney, built his own villa, Chateau d'If, in Randwick, and died there in 1910 of cirrhosis of the liver.

Johann Augustus Bernard Koch arrived with his family in Melbourne in 1855 aged fifteen. In 1870 he is listed as architect in Richmond and over the next thirty years he designed sixty

Vahland's Mechanics Institute and School of Mining and Industries is today Bendigo's TAFE College.

buildings there – he was appointed city architect in 1887 – and in Hawthorn. His projects included the two Richmond libraries, the Women's, Melbourne and Castlemaine hospitals, and the Melbourne Corn Exchange. Two of his Richmond hotels, the Spread Eagle and the Prince Alfred, have survived, as well as some warehouses, factories and stables.

In Perth, Friedrich Wilhelm Gustav Liebe left an impressive legacy of magnificent Victorian buildings. He was born in Wittenberg, Saxony in 1862 and had obtained a building diploma at the Vienna Technical School. Liebe arrived in Adelaide in 1886 and, after a short spell as a builder in South Australia and Melbourne, came to Perth in 1891. Here he built not only homes but also a large number of public buildings, including the Art Gallery and His Majesty's Theatre, the Queen's Hall, and the Dowerin and Moora Hotel – credited with having been one of the most lavish in Western Australia.[35]

Then there were the wine-growers. One of the earliest wine entrepreneurs was Friedrich Wilhelm Christian Luther, a descendant of Martin Luther. As his father was well off, he received university education, but he had to leave Germany after fatally wounding a fellow student in a duel at Heidelberg. Luther came to Australia in 1838 and after a brief period in Sydney worked as a manager for

Menkens's Middle Wood Chambers, Scott Street, Newcastle, built in 1892

the Ogilvy family near the Oaks, to the southwest of Sydney. By the 1850s he had amassed sufficient capital to purchase his own property nearby – The Hermitage – where he cultivated grapevines and citrus fruits. He died at the age of fifty-four while working in the orchard, and was survived by his wife, five sons and two daughters. Numerous Luthers today live in the Bathurst-Oberon district, and The Hermitage has been preserved as a magnificent monument to the pioneering days.

In South Australia, Johann Gramp established the Orlando vineyard in 1847, and four years later Joseph Ernst Seppelt started the Seppeltsfield vineyard in the Barossa. Seppelt was born in

Wüstewaltersdorf in Lower Silesia in 1813, the son of a tobacco, snuff and liquor producer. Because of a decline in his family's business, he decided to emigrate to South Australia with his wife, Johanna Charlotte, and their three children in 1849. His wine-growing turned into a most profitable business. He suffered delirium tremens and died suddenly in January 1868. Joseph was succeeded in the business by his son, Oscar Benno Pedro Seppelt, who maintained the Seppelt company as one of Australia's leading wine producers. The well-known Craigmoor Estate in the Mudgee wine region of New South Wales was founded in 1859 by Adam Roth, who had emigrated to Australia in 1857. He named his estate Rothview, a name changed by his grandson in 1935 to Craigmoor winery. Other German wine producers achieved fame in their time but failed to establish a family tradition. Winzer wine grown in the Rutherglen district of Victoria late in the nineteenth century, for example, had the highest reputation of all wines marketed in Melbourne.

In the light of Germany's age-old beer brewing tradition it is not surprising that Central Europeans contributed greatly to the development of brewing in Australia. Edmund Resch arrived from Dortmund with his brothers Emil and Richard in 1863. They mined copper in Cobar – the first to do so – and in 1877 Edmund and Richard started the Lyon Brewery in Wilcannia. Obviously stationhands, drovers and shearers provided a constant clientele at Wilcannia, which ranks with Bourke and Walgett as the three hottest towns in New South Wales. Business was so good that Edmund was able to buy a brewery in Sydney in 1896, laying the foundation for Resch's Brewery – and Resch's Pilsener was for a century one of New South Wales's most popular beers.

Most famous of the nineteenth-century German artists was Austrian Eugene von Guérard. He was born in 1812 and educated as an artist at the Düsseldorf Kunstakademie. It is said, however, that the sentimentality of the Düsseldorf school was not entirely to his liking, and he preferred to follow the pattern set by scientists – to go far afield and explore. He came to Australia in the wake of the gold rush but soon found that his talent as a painter provided a more reliable income. Until his return to Europe in 1882 he ran a painting school in Melbourne and was for several years the director of the National School of Art and the curator of the National Gallery of Victoria. While in Australia he produced a large number of lithographs and oil paintings of the Snowy Mountains, the goldfields and other areas in the southeast, and his compassionate portrayal of Aborigines has earned

Resch's Brewery at Waverley in Sydney (Powerhouse Museum, Sydney)

him great praise.[36] Hans Heysen, born in 1877 in Hamburg, began his long and successful career in the 1890s by painting the country that surrounded Hahndorf.

But it was above all in music that Germans excelled. There are records of two German choral societies in Adelaide in the 1840s – the Deutsche Liedertafel and the Adelaider Liedertafel – and Carl Linger, a Berlin-born and educated conductor-composer who arrived in the colony in August 1848, is credited as being the first German to leave a permanent imprint on South Australian music. Others who played an important part in Adelaide's early musical life include Theodore Heidecke, leader of the Catholic and Volunteer bands, and the Hamburg-born Christian Reimers, whose music was said to be 'thoroughly original'. Contemporaries maintained that he 'has probably few, if any equals', and the sweet sounds of his cello 'have often been heard by large and admiring audiences in our Town Hall'.[37] Carl Püttmann, son of Hermann Püttman, became a teacher in piano, violin and singing, and in 1867 the conductor of the Adelaider Liedertafel – with whom in 1870 he produced his first opera, *Morgenbruch* (early dawn). Immanuel Gotthold Reinmann established the Adelaide College of Music in 1883, which became a focal point of German musicians in the city. Other prominent musicians of nineteenth-century South Australia include the pianist, conductor and composer Moritz Heuzenrode, and the Brunswick-born pianist Carl Julius Bertram. August Moritz Heinecke, born in Dresden in 1863, was already at the age of sixteen the first violinist of the Royal Dresden Court Opera. He arrived in Adelaide in 1890 and was soon put in charge of the College of Music. Heinecke maintained his prominent position until the outbreak of war in 1914. His Grand Orchestra included numerous German musicians.[38]

As we might expect, with Queensland receiving the largest share of German immigration, Germans formed the core of professional players in Brisbane. Violinist Julius Kopp became the leader of the Queensland Theatre Ensemble and the conductor of the Brisbane Liedertafel. Otto Linden conducted the Brisbane Philharmonic Society and Andrew Siegel the Queensland Volunteer Band. 'These German musicians came from families with generations of musical experience', writes a historian of the colony, 'and they brought with them traditions of musical craft unequalled outside their homeland'. Unfortunately, the colony did not appreciate their talents and many left to perform elsewhere.[39]

In Victoria, Carl Gottlieb Elsasser arrived from Württemberg in 1853 and spent the rest of his life in Melbourne as a music teacher, conductor and composer, as did Julius Siede from Dresden. Siede became the conductor of the Melbourne Deutsche Liedertafel in 1872 and the president of the Melbourne Musical Association of Victoria in 1879. When this body merged with the Musical Society of Victoria, he became its vice-president. His career ended in 1889 because of ill health, and according to the *Australian Dictionary of Biography* the Liedertafel 'in an unprecedented gesture' raised £491 for him in tribute to 'his blameless professional and private life and that public respect that he commanded'. Soprano Ilma de Murska, of German origin, drew large audiences in Melbourne, and so did the famous violinist Johannes Secundus Kruse. In New South Wales, Karl Kreschmann is listed as a successful violinist and conductor.

Outside the professional scene, all towns and cities, indeed all rural settlements with any significant number of Germans, had their *Gesangverein* (choral societies), and the street musicians who busked in the buzzing centres of the capital cities came predominantly from Central Europe.

German immigrants or their descendants participated in local councils everywhere they settled, but only in South Australia and Queensland, the two most German colonies, did many make it to the colonial parliaments. We have met Adolf Heinrich Bartels, Mayor of Adelaide between 1871 to 1873, and before him was Walter Tiedemann from 1865. Johann Heinz became the Mayor of Ballarat in 1889 and a few years later Karl Fraenkel became Mayor of Bunbury in Western Australia. South Australia elected ten men of German origin to the parliament, of whom one, Martin Basedow, briefly held the portfolio of Education Minister in 1881. Robert Homburg served as Attorney-General from 1890 to 1895 and was the first non-British appointee to the Supreme Court of South Australia, in 1905. There were eight German members of parliament in Queensland, and Johann Christian Heussler held the offices of Acting Chairman of Committees and Acting President of the Legislative Council. To the best of my knowledge only one German politician made it to parliament in New South Wales (Bernard Holtermann, 1882).

In Victoria, Otto Sachse was elected to the Legislative Assembly in 1892, and in 1902 Maximilian Hirsch won the seat of Mandurang. Hirsch arrived in 1890 from Ceylon, where he had been a coffee planter and a (successful) political agitator for the abolition of the rice tax. He soon held a prominent position in the anti-tariff party, and was a keen supporter of improved conditions for workers and of female suffrage. No one of German origin reached prominence in Tasmanian politics or in the Australian labour movement, although the father of Australia's first Labor prime minister, J. C. Watson, was German. There were socialists in Adelaide's Allgemeiner Deutscher Verein and in the Verein Vorwärts in Melbourne, but their political leanings were not popular with the (non-Marxist) British-based Australian labour movement.

German clubs sprang up in all capital cities, industrial and mining centres, and all other places with a high German population. In the nineteenth century they served essentially to maintain – or at least provide reminiscences of – the customs and traditions of their original *Heimat*, although by the turn of the century this relatively harmless club life was being undermined by the arrival of *Deutschtumspolitik*.[40]

Newspapers tried to encourage German customs while also paying attention to the day-to-day affairs of their adopted country. *Australische Zeitung*, under the ownership of Martin Basedow, stood out for its skilled journalism and competent economic management. Basedow arrived in South Australia in April 1848 from a small town near

Members of the Marburg German Club (John Oxley Library, State Library of Queensland)

Hamburg where he had taught at the local grammar school. In 1850 he opened a Lutheran school in Tanunda, described ten years later as the best German school in the colony. In 1863 he established the *Tanunda Deutsche Zeitung*, having been for several years part-owner of the previous *Süd-Australische Zeitung*. The name was changed in 1870 to *Australische Deutsche Zeitung* and in 1874 Basedow moved to Adelaide, where he and his father-in-law, Carl Muecke, joined to form *Australische Zeitung*, the most successful German paper in Australia until its closure in 1917. From 1876 to 1890 Basedow represented the Barossa in the House of Assembly; as is indicated by his brief stint as Minister for Education, he was a particularly keen educator and worked tirelessly to improve the South Australian education system.[41]

Newspapers in Sydney and Melbourne did not do so well. In 1855 Hermann Püttmann and Johann Kruse founded the *Deutsche Monatsschrift* in Sydney, but the paper soon folded – as did several newspapers in Melbourne that Püttmann brought out in the early 1860s, and Detogardi's paper in Sydney. But in Queensland the

Nordaustralische Zeitung (1876–1903) and later the *Queenslander Herald* (1895–1939) were more successful. By extolling 'a form of *"Deutschtum"* (Germanism) that ensured that the readers' "sentimental" attachment to the ancestral soil of the Fatherland did not conflict with fidelity to the British crown', these papers managed to keep the German-speaking population in touch with political, social and cultural events in Australia and overseas.[42]

German immigration had peaked by 1890 – a result of economic and political change in Germany and of the 1890s depression in most Australian colonies. Only 4000 new migrants are estimated to have arrived between 1890 and 1914. This means that people of German origin accounted for some 10–12 per cent of the population of Queensland and South Australia by the beginning of the twentieth century, 4–5 per cent in Victoria, and a little less in New South Wales. In Western Australia the number of German-born peaked in 1911, when the Census listed 2036 – in addition to 1280 settlers who listed Austria-Hungary as their birthplace (most Austro-Hungarians were listed as Croatians, but the ethnic pluralism of the Habsburg Empire ensured that the dividing lines were very thin). Small as these numbers may seem, they suffice to establish that the 1788–1914 history of Australia was not an exclusively British affair.

6

THE SHADOW YEARS

Imperial Germany, *Weltpolitik* and Australia

Just months after the Berlin Wall had come down and the two
Germanys were preparing their reunification, the doyen of German
writers, Günter Grass, argued in 1990 that a reunited Germany was
in no one's interests. In his opinion 'nobody with a common sense
and memory of the past' would again allow a massive concentration
of power in the centre of Europe. Neither the victorious powers of
World War II, nor the Poles, French, Dutch or Danes, nor indeed the
Germans themselves, would want such a state to emerge again. There
should be no recreation of the united Germany that under a succession of rulers over less than seventy-five years had 'managed to write
into our history books a tale of misery forced on others and ourselves,
of devastation, loss, millions of refugees, millions of deaths and the
burden of insurmountable crimes'.

Grass's remarks were not appreciated in Germany. He was seen
as a killjoy, spoiling the excitement of the divided nation coming
together after a long separation, and experts were called upon to
correct the writer and set the facts straight. But because Grass was
held in high esteem – not much later, he was ranked first among
the top 100 German intellectuals by the respectable *Frankfurter All-
gemeine Zeitung* – qualms remained about such a comment from a
high profile thinker who had a reputation for shaking the national
conscience with occasionally unwelcome criticism. With the benefit
of hindsight, Grass's worry that the reunited Germany might again

revert to the expansionist policies of its ancestors proved unjustified. The enlarged Federal Republic has continued the constructive policies of pre-unification times, working peacefully towards the enlargement of the European Union on the international level, and consolidating the nation's democratic principles and institutions domestically. But it is not difficult to see why Grass felt uneasy about the German past: marked by war and aggression from its inception, the story of the German Reich is not a happy one.

Fürst Otto von Bismarck, appointed prime minister by the Prussian king in 1862 to deal with an obstructionist Prussian parliament (*Landtag*) that had repeatedly refused to vote for increased military expenditure, and the man who, more than anyone else, was behind the creation of the German Empire in 1871, told the parliamentarians at their first meeting that 'The great questions of the day are not decided by speeches and majority decisions . . . but by iron and blood'. Bismarck lived up to his principles. Relying on rule by Royal emergency decree, which sidelined the Prussian lower house, he wrested the northern duchies of Schleswig-Holstein from Denmark in a short unequal war in 1864. The Austrian Empire, which had joined Prussia in this shady enterprise, received its due reward when Bismarck turned on them in a second 'unification war' two years later. Although supported by all other German states, the Austrians lost the decisive battle at Königgrätz in July 1866. This brought the whole of northern Germany under direct Prussian control.

The victims of Bismarckian power politics included the Kingdom of Hanover, thus bringing to an end the centuries-old rule of the proud House of Hanover. Like most of Hesse, Hanover became a Prussian province. In 1870, aided by inept diplomacy on the part of the government of Emperor Napoleon III, Bismarck manipulated a war with France and managed to rally the southern German states behind the Prussian adventure. As in the war with Austria, Prussian superior rifle power won the decisive battles, and on 18 January 1871 in the Hall of Mirrors at Versailles the German Empire was proclaimed. The Prussian king became the 'German emperor' and Bismarck the Reich's first chancellor. Enthusiasm in the southern states of Bavaria, Württemberg and Baden for the newly created empire was limited. France had to cede the provinces of Alsace-Lorraine to Germany, in addition to paying a huge indemnity. As a leading work on the rise of Nazism recently put it:

Military force and military action created the Reich; and in doing so they swept aside legitimate institutions, redrew state boundaries and overthrew long-established traditions, with a radicalism and ruthlessness that cast a shadow over the subsequent development of Germany. They also thereby legitimized the use of force for political ends to a degree well beyond what was common in most other countries.[1]

The unification of Germany ended Bismarck's spell of aggressive foreign policies, but his peaceful conduct of international diplomacy in the following years was not mirrored on the domestic scene, where the Iron Chancellor, judged to have been 'a hater of unique ingenuity and stamina',[2] soon turned against 'dissenters' inside the Reich. Catholics were the first victims, followed by the socialists. His fierce persecution of the German Social Democratic Party, however, proved his undoing. The new Kaiser, Wilhelm II, who had ascended to the throne in 1888 and who wanted peace in his Reich, dismissed Bismarck in 1890.

Regrettably, the departure of the ageing statesman improved neither imperial Germany's domestic policies nor its foreign policies. By the 1890s aggressive and expansionist ideas had spread to large sections of the German middle classes which, together with the governments that succeeded Bismarck, had become convinced that Germany was being denied its rightful role in world affairs. The German nation had done poorly in the colonial carve-up of the globe and it was mandatory to correct this state of affairs: Germany must ascend to the rank of a *Weltmacht* (world power). To repeat the much-cited comment to the German Reichstag by the Foreign Secretary and later Imperial Chancellor, Bernard von Bülow, Germany demanded its 'place under the sun'. Such ideas were broadly popular and were heralded by organisations such as the Pan-German League, the Association for Germandom Abroad and the Navy League (*Flottenverein*). The Navy League alone had a membership of well over 300 000.

Most fateful for the twentieth century was the decision of the German imperial government, enthusiastically supported by a wide swathe of the middle class, to embark upon a massive construction program for a German navy. At the time of the unification of Germany, the German navy was rated second class; it consisted of a small number of ships deemed necessary to protect coasts and harbour facilities in the North and Baltic seas. On the eve of war in 1914 the German battle fleet was second in size only to that of the United Kingdom. It is not easy to find a rational explanation for this huge increase. The broad belief in free trade that had marked the Age of Imperialism meant that the rapidly expanding German export trade did not need large-scale military protection. And as far as German colonies were concerned, whereas a small number of individuals and a few companies may have benefited from the enterprise, imperial possessions in Africa and the Pacific were generally a financial liability. As we now know, the explanation for the disastrous *Flottenpolitik* lies in the (irrational) Social Darwinism that had gripped parts of Europe, and Germany in particular, around the turn of the century. The man in charge of the German battle-fleet, Alfred von Tirpitz, was a most dogmatic and determinist Social Darwinist, convinced that Germany's economic, demographic and economic expansion would inevitably lead to a military show-down with the world's foremost imperial power – the United Kingdom. This view had widespread support in educated German circles, including the great majority of pastors in the United Evangelical Church.

By 1911 it had become clear that the *Flottenpolitik* was an abysmal failure. Enormous investments had been poured into a hole – the arms and steel manufacturer Krupps making the only (but massive) profits. Concerns that in case of war the German Empire would have to fight on both the western and eastern fronts shifted the emphasis in military planning from the navy back to the army. A huge increase in the German field forces caused another arms race, and by 1912 the idea of preventive warfare had firmly gripped the army's leadership. Whether the civilian administration agreed with such a bellicose strategy has been subject to debate ever since. The fact remains that when the showdown occurred in the summer of 1914, after the assassination of the Austrian Crown Prince at Sarajevo, the army's Supreme Command prevailed; the Schlieffen Plan, which turned the war from a localised conflict in the Balkans into a full European war, was put into effect on 4 August 1914.[3] Any doubts the political leadership may have had about the army's preventive capacity were soon set aside. German war aims announced in the September program of 1914 had the support of the government, the military leadership, and Germany's industrial and agrarian tycoons.[4] They all stood firm on the war aims until the autumn of 1918, when they stared defeat in the face.

Australia first became involved in Germany's nascent *Weltpolitik* in November 1884, when marines hoisted the German flag at various locations in northeastern New Guinea and adjacent islands. This was the beginning of the Imperial Colony of German New Guinea – as the German protectorates in the Pacific were officially called – which eventually encompassed a territory covering approximately

9000 square kilometres of the Pacific Ocean, from New Guinea in the west to Samoa in the east. The German arrival to the north soured Australian–German relations. The Queensland government, worried about a growing German presence in the region, had attempted to take possession of New Guinea in April 1883, but this was overruled at the insistence of the British prime minister, William Gladstone, allegedly because of the prevalent racist bias of most of Queensland's white population.[5] This was the beginning of Australia's lingering resentment and distrust of German imperialism, which was to increase dramatically when the German cruiser squadron set up a permanent base at Kiachow Bay on China's northern seaboard.

The Tirpitz Plan envisaged that the decisive battle for world supremacy would be fought between Britain and the German Empire with big battleships in the waters of the Atlantic, in particular the North Sea. However, the cruiser squadron and its auxiliary vessels were to give important assistance by pinning down the British Empire's forces in the Australasian / East Asian region. It was expected that not only would German war vessels inflict considerable damage on enemy trade and on troop transports to Europe, but that direct naval actions against Australian and New Zealand harbour facilities and coastal towns would unsettle the region and hence further destabilise the Allied war effort. A massive war intelligence system was to prepare and direct German military actions in the East Asia / Western Pacific region.[6] The extent to which military and intelligence networks in Australia were aware of the German plans is not known. However, security agents did not need to be close relatives of Sherlock Holmes or pre-Cold War agent 007 James Bond to work out what the massive German arms build-up to the north of Australia meant. This explains the sensitivity of Australian authorities when war broke out, and the fact that consulates and associated bodies were high on the list of priorities. Their suspicions were well justified.

The poor fate of Deutschtum

In a conference held in the mid-1990s on German–Australian relations, one of the contributors noted that 'with the creation of the German Reich came the imperial consulates who took the utmost care to make it clear that they presented a great European power'.[7] This is a very diplomatic assessment of the role and work of imperial German consuls in Australia who, as chief proponents of *Deutschtum* abroad – not to mince words – carried on in the years of *Weltpolitik* like the proverbial bull in the china shop. Whereas before unification the work of (honorary) consuls was restricted to traditional areas such as trade, commerce and immigration, the professional diplomatic system of Wilhelmine Germany stood out for its high level of politicisation.

The chief venue for the propagation of pan-German ideas was the annual Nationalfest held in Sydney to celebrate the anniversary of the German Empire's foundation on 18 January 1871. Under the auspices of the consulate-general, who was also in charge of the event's organisation and content, year after year the gospel of *Deutschtumspolitik* was proclaimed loud and clear. Banners carried slogans such as 'With God for Kaiser and Fatherland' and 'We Germans only fear God, but nothing else in this world'. And enthusiastic speeches were made in praise of the proud German ships which, 'passing through the world's seas are the most imposing and fastest'; likewise, the 'awe-inspiring German Navy', another proud achievement of the newly created Reich, will not only protect the ever-growing German trade but will also lend protection to all Germans abroad.[8] This comment from an excited observer of the 1906 Nationalfest sums up the spirit:

> To all the excitement is suddenly added the sound of gunfire, 'spread out' is the order given. We can hardly step aside before a group of navy youngsters storms in, dressed in white, flattering suits – with guns, at the double, march, march – they pass us. A pretty sight these young fellows, sons of German countrymen, which greatly add to the festival with their 'military' performance.[9]

The aim of the Nationalfest was not only to impress the German nationals but also to win over the traditional German community, i.e. the descendants of the German immigrants, to the cause of *Deutschtum*. It was motivated by the view of the *Deutschtums-Apostels* that these German communities had lost their proper sense of nationhood. Visits by consuls-general and high-ranking navy officers to such centres of German settlement as the Barossa, the Riverina, and the Logan Valley revealed sobering news about the persistence of Germandom. The Lutheran churches were still there, and in some cases their schools; there still might be *Musikvereine*, *Turnvereine* (gymnastic clubs) skittle clubs (nine-pin bowling clubs), rifle clubs and *Skatbrüder* associations – but the people here were Australians. Of German origin no doubt, but Australian nevertheless. And when in 1903 officers and sailors called upon the Allgemeiner Deutscher Verein in Adelaide, they noted with horror that the pictures that decorated the club walls were not of Wilhelm II but of leading German socialists. John Moses sums it up:

The cover of a program for the celebration of Germany's national day in Sydney, 17 January 1914; the caption reads, 'We want to be Germans as our fathers were'

A German rally at Highfield, near Toowoomba, c.1910

as loyal servants of the Wilhelmine power elite they shared the
common assumptions about the superiority of German 'Kultur',
especially over Anglo-Saxon civilisation . . . But although these highly
educated and otherwise rational officials could analyse statistics
and even acknowledge that 'Deutschtum' was virtually doomed to
extinction, they still clung defiantly to the belief that somehow it was
of crucial importance to keep fostering it . . . [hence] . . . instead of
using the occasion to promote German Australian cordiality, the
Consuls General encouraged it as an opportunity to infuse into the
German-Australians a decidedly Pan German spirit. This can only be
attributed to the 'unspoken assumption' that sooner or later a kind of
social Darwinistic struggle for world domination would have to take
place between the ageing, moribund and essentially frivolous British
civilization and the youthful, vigorous and spiritually superior
German Empire.[10]

In the final years of peace the Nationalfest attracted as many as
3000 visitors, which shows that the majority of German citizens, and
to a lesser degree some Germans who were naturalised Australians,
sympathised with and supported *Deutschtumspolitik*. This should be
kept in mind when considering the fate of the German community
in Australia. Nevertheless, the perversion of *Deutschtum* from a kind
of traditional peasant-style *Gemütlichkeit* to a militarist, aggressive
nationalism had no real following among the Australians of German
descent. The reasons are obvious. Because of their cultural, ethnic and
racial affinity, German – 'racial cousins' is the term sometimes used –
migrants both in the nineteenth and later in the twentieth century integrated very rapidly into their Australian host environment. All accounts
concur that the process of assimilation usually took no longer than one
generation. This was not due to pressure from – or policies designed
by – the Australian authorities, but was a natural process.

Migrants, and their children even more so, had to learn English to
advance in life and to conduct most of their day-to-day business. Peer-
group pressure and intermarriage contributed, as did economic reality.
The anglicising of family names occurred well before the Great War
(although its outbreak in 1914 hastened the process), and German first
names soon gave way to local ones. The Thiess family for example, of
one of Australia's largest industrial and mining companies, dates back
to 'settlers of solid German farming stock at the old town of Drayton
on the Darling Downs'. Nevertheless, by the early twentieth century
their sons' names were not Fritz, Franz, Rolf or Theodor but Cecil, Pat,

Bert, Stan and Les.[11] And although some Germans – a minority – did maintain the traditional German *Gemütlichkeit*, most 'Australianised' their way of life: they followed the horses, played cricket in summer, and in winter Australian Rules if they lived in the southern states, or rugby in New South Wales and Queensland. Only the small, isolated Lutheran villages in South Australia are said to have maintained German customs and language. But this belief, too, may need more thorough study to be substantiated. To judge by the numerous prewar South Australian Sheffield Shield cricketers of rural German background, that state seems not to have differed greatly from the rest.[12]

The position of German schools had declined well before 1914. Although by the turn of the century there were still 48 German schools officially listed in South Australia, approximately 40 in Queensland, 10 in Victoria and one in New South Wales – all of them primary schools – enrolment was low and many had become Sunday schools. The two attempts, in Melbourne and Sydney, to set up secondary *Gymnasium*-type grammar schools were short-lived. The great majority of German parents sent their children to state schools, which were free and where they were taught by trained teachers – or, if they were more affluent, to the prestigious private schools. Again the reasons are obvious. Living in an English environment they had to be instructed according to the states' curricula in order not to be disadvantaged.

Deutschtum did manage to get a foothold in some of the more prominent associations, such as the Concordia Club in Sydney or the Tivoli Club in Melbourne, in the years before the war – because so many of their members were late arrivals. This led to confrontations with second- and third-generation Germans who, though Australians by now, were proud of their German background but refused to be drawn into the politicisation brought about by *Weltpolitik*. But nowhere did members with pan-German tendencies take over the established clubs. Moreover, the ratio of club members to the overall German population was low. The Concordia Club in Sydney, the wealthiest and most successful, had 230 members in 1906 – 2 to 3 per cent of Sydney's German population. As Ian Harmstorf has correctly pointed out, those more integrated into Anglo-Australian society felt neither the need nor the compulsion to participate in German social or cultural events, or the necessity to maintain their mother tongue.[13]

It was in the Lutheran churches that the German language survived the longest. This had nothing to do with the propagation of *Deutschtum* but was due to the long-held view that the Lutheran faith could only be expressed properly in German. This practice, however, had run into dire straits by the turn of the twentieth century.[14] Plans to set up a Lutheran training centre in South Australia were cut short by the outbreak of war but recommenced soon after hostilities had stopped, when the Immanuel Synod set up a seminary in Adelaide. Nevertheless, politicisation of German society did not stop at the church doors. If anything, the opposite was the case:

> Quite consciously they [the pastors] were going to change the established rules of international relations because of a commitment to a peculiarly German philosophy of history and politics and, one could add, theology of state. There was hardly a pastor or theologian who did not believe in Germany's God-given right to expand, by force if necessary, at the expense of putatively inferior and moribund cultures of the other Great powers, especially Britain, because it was demonstrably the will of Almighty God.[15]

Patriotic Prussian pastors advocating *Deutschtum* and *Weltpolitik* were not desired in organisations that from the beginning took a strong apolitical stance, and English-speaking Lutheran pastors from the United States had begun to arrive by the late nineteenth century. Germandom in Australia may not have been a dead duck, but it was a very lame one. Those who believe that 1914–1918 marks the abrupt termination of a flourishing German cultural scene, brought about by Australian malevolence, overlook some important factors.

World War I: myth and reality

When war broke out in August 1914, Australia was prepared. Army units quickly overran the German station in New Guinea, and New Zealand the one in Western Samoa. At sea, Australian and New Zealand harbours, as well as coastal regions, were closely watched to enable quick action against German vessels in the event of hostilities. Defence capacities had been increased and the newly created Royal Australian Navy possessed some powerful modern weapons: the dreadnought *Australia* alone sufficed as a deterrent for major naval warfare. The early destruction of the telegraph station on Yap by the British warship *Minotaur* was a decisive blow to the German communication system, and many German steamers, unaware of the news, sailed blithely into Allied ports or were impounded before they could depart. In the first days of war 23 German vessels, ranging from 4000 to 7000 tonnes, were seized in British and Allied harbours, and in the end 26 ships were detained in Australian waters alone. Moreover, the Japanese entry into the war on the Allied side meant that Germany's major war base in the region, Tsingtao in northern China, could not be held. Thus the main body of the cruiser squadron headed for the Atlantic, but was destroyed on the way by superior British forces near the Falkland Islands. Nevertheless, a small number of German vessels, above all the legendary *Emden*, continued warfare in the region until 1917.

On the domestic scene, security authorities had tightened their intelligence system, and suspicious characters were kept under surveillance and arrested on the outbreak of war. Consulates, consular staff and people or institutions with close connections to them were at the top of the list, as were particularly vociferous advocates of *Deutschtum* and German nationals liable for military service. In Brisbane, the imperial German consul, Dr Eugen Hirschfeld, who had been among the most active Kaiser and Fatherland enthusiasts in Australia, was interned immediately after the war started, as was the editor of the *Queensländer Herald*, Frederick Monzel. Unfortunately, the 'pious peasant obscurantist' and politically harmless form of Germandom cultivated by the leader of the German Apostolic Church in Queensland, H. F. Niemeyer, was misunderstood by the authorities, and he too was interned.[16]

Regular visits of German warships to Adelaide would have contributed to the fact that the offices of leading businessman and BHP chairman Carl Muecke, who was also the German consul, were raided in November 1914 (there was also the fact that BHP and other Australian metal firms had sold lead, copper and zinc to Germany[17] – and everyone knew that the material was used for wartime purposes). No incriminating evidence was found, but nevertheless Muecke remained on the South Australian list of suspicious characters, partly because of his rigorous denial of German war crimes. Among the early internees were pastors of the Prussian Evangelical Church – not generally known for their imperviousness to Germany's world mission – who had been sent from Berlin to preach in a number of Australian congregations. But most internees were German nationals who were now citizens, and potential soldiers, of an enemy country.

By 1915 the joint impact of the Gallipoli disaster with its huge losses, the use of poison gas at Ypres, the sinking of the *Lusitania* and the news of German atrocities against civilians in Belgium and France – sadly, not all mere propaganda[18] – was being felt. Germanophobia directed against Australia's German communities became more pronounced in political circles and in sections of the media, and led to a series of capricious and indiscriminate acts by Australian authorities and members of the general public. These stories have been well covered, and clearly account for the lion's share of the topic 'Germans in Australia 1914–1918', but are still worth commenting on here. The worst incident occurred in the Torrens Island internment camp, where two internees, a German and a Swede, were flogged for half an hour with a cat-o'-nine-tails for trying to escape. Prisoners protested and the German government threatened reprisals against Australian prisoners of war unless conditions at Torrens Island improved. The officer in charge, Captain Hawkers, who had become notorious for brutality against prisoners, was demoted to the ranks and the camp was closed two months later. Then there were the cases of Eduard Kaempffer, Carl Ernst and August Schmidt, who had their property confiscated on shady legal grounds.

Appalling, too, was the case of Matilda Rockstroh, postmistress at the St Kilda Road post office, who had been in the public service for thirty-seven years. Her parents had emigrated to Australia in the middle of the nineteenth century and Matilda was born in Australia. Although a subsequent investigation found no evidence of disloyalty, the officer in charge nevertheless came to this conclusion:

> her close lineal connection with the German race and her long social and domestic association with her own German relations and friends makes it unlikely that her inclinations and proclivities, if they could be discovered, and put to an enforced election, would tend towards the interests of the British Empire as against those of her own race.[19]

Although Miss Rockstroh lost her position as postmistress, she was allowed to remain in the public service. In this, she was more fortunate than H. H. Clausen, a linesman for the General Post Office in Brisbane, who was dismissed because 'Physiognomically his Teutonic origin is striking'.[20] Clausen had arrived in Australia as a child and was forty-one at the time of the inquiry.

In Western Australia, the Cabinet passed the Public Servant Act, forcing people who had at any time been subjects of an enemy country to retire, and a number of German bakers were put out of work because of pressure from the Amalgamated Baking Trades Industrial Union.[21] And there was petty chicanery. South Australia's attorney-general, Herman Homburg, who could not be suspected of the slightest enemy sympathy, had an armed guard placed outside his office; Sydney brewer Edmund Resch had one placed outside his house. At

A cartoon from the Bulletin, *1915*

Beagle Bay the German Pallottine fathers had their fingerprints taken and there were demands to close down the mission, which was said to threaten Australia's security. But it took little effort from Archbishop Clune in Perth to have such absurd claims dismissed. The missionaries had their correspondence censored and their movement supervised at times. But they decided not to pursue blame and used the war years to construct a new and beautiful church.

Historians are right, and indeed it is their duty, to draw attention to such practices and to highlight them as negative aspects of Australian history. But they have an equal duty to stay clear of gross generalising and not to fall for a *Pauschalverurteilung* (a collective condemnation) of Australian authorities or the Australian people. The number of Germans who were directly affected by wartime measures

The Holsworthy Internment Camp near Liverpool, New South Wales (Australian War Memorial, Canberra, H 17349).

or other fall-out from the war was small. Of the approximately 150 000 second-, third- and even fourth-generation descendants of nineteenth-century immigrants, and the approximately 25 000 naturalised German-Australians, 61 were interned. This small number itself undermines claims of widespread arbitrary arrests and internments.

No doubt there were cases of injustice. The internment of William Ruhno, a successful businessman in southeastern Queensland who was held on false charges of intimidating the German community, is a serious indictment of leading intelligence officers.[22] But not all Australians of German ancestry were innocent victims of malevolent security officers. Although Dr Friedrich Wilhelm August Finselbach from Temora was in the prewar years the keenest *Deutschtum* enthusiast, he escaped the first round of detention. However, when he attempted to send detailed material about a proposed naval base at Port Stephens to Switzerland, with the request that it be forwarded to Mr Kiliani, the last German consul-general in Australia, he was arrested and interned for the rest of the war.

Many German-born Australians had difficulties coping with the fact that their new country was at war with their homeland, and found it hard to stomach the prevalent anti-German atmosphere. This led to unwise actions. Thus it was foolish for signwriter Jacob Rumph, for example, to paint the whole front of his shop in Perth with red, yellow and black (imperial Germany's colours) and to write in large letters, 'The Anzac Dyer and Cleaner'. And Mrs Carlshausen, owner of the wine saloon in Beaufort Street, Perth, was not acting in her own best interests when she wrote to her son that her best wishes were with Germany and the Germans, who 'thank God are well advanced', while the English on the other hand 'can bite their back bone if they could because they don't know how it would end with the war' – and the same goes for the Australians, who 'will wake up if they have to stand face-to-face with a modern German soldier'.[23] Difficult as it may have been, it would have been better not to rock the boat in the emotionally charged atmosphere of the war.

The case of Dr Maximilian Hertz is another example of injudicious behaviour. At the outbreak of war, Hertz was a successful physician/surgeon. He was greatly perturbed that his new country was at war with his homeland and found it very hard to accept the prevailing anti-German atmosphere. He expressed his feelings in a number of letters, which were intercepted, and a diary, which was later confiscated by the censors. Hertz was interned and spent the war years at Trial Bay. After the war he became the target of a particularly nasty campaign by the Australian branch of the British Medical Association to have him deported to Germany. They probably wished to settle old scores: Hertz had severely criticised the standards of the Australian medical profession at various prewar conferences.[24]

The overwhelming majority (90 per cent) of the 5688 people interned in Australia were *Reichsdeutsche* (subjects of imperial Germany).[25] As reservists in the German army, they had to expect to face the consequences of their government's policy to lead Europe into war. Harsh as internment was, it was nothing compared to the fate that would have awaited them had they managed to get back in time to fulfil their military duties. The apocalyptic horror of trench warfare meant that they stood a good chance of either being blown to pieces, or dying some other ghastly death, or emerging from the war blind, crippled or insane. As a more thoughtful analyst of the domestic situation in Australia 1914–1918 aptly commented:

> A government's duty is to protect its territory and people. From the
> beginning of the war, the Commonwealth had an increased
> responsibility to take measures to that end. Those measures included

Villa Frieda, a hut made from corrugated iron by German prisoners of war at Berrima, New South Wales.

protection against known or expected dangers, and precautions against possible dangers. In my view the government did not have to wait for an external threat to materialize, or for sabotage or espionage to be carried out, before acting. If strife loomed, the Commonwealth had to be able to identify enemy aliens quickly, and know where they were, and what they were doing . . . it had a responsibility to take preventive action.[26]

Indeed, given the enormous strain the war placed on people and society, acts of sabotage could not be ruled out and did occur. On New Year's Day 1915 Mulla Abdulla and Mahomed Gool, both of Muslim faith, decided to support the war effort of the Ottoman Empire and fired at a miners' picnic train at Broken Hill. Four people were killed and scores were injured. In response, an angry group of people, unable to get hold of Turks, burnt down the German Club. Times of war create great tensions for societies and individuals. Mulla Abdulla and Mahomed Gool were law-abiding, peaceful citizens before August 1914; three months later they felt that they had to sacrifice their lives for the sultan. The authorities' precautionary measures ensured that their killing rampage remained an isolated event in Australia. Protection of its civilian population is the first duty of a government, and to have failed to do so at this time would have been not only negligent but criminal.[27]

What really happened as far as the great majority of Australia's German were concerned? A look at some of the many recent local studies of German settlements throws light on the topic. In their work in Grafton and the Clarence River district in northern New South Wales, Geoffrey Burckhardt and Nola Mackay found that 'throughout 1915 the German families here carried out their civic duties and their employment, conducting their business without interference'. But in Lismore on Christmas Eve of that year, probably aroused by articles in Sydney newspapers, 'a drunken mob was incited to march on shops and businesses held by "foreigners"', causing damage to a number of premises. Soon police arrived, however, and arrested five of the rioters, charging them with disturbing public peace and with unlawfully damaging public property. The local *Daily Examiner* published a scathing article about the 'half drunken hoodlums' and their actions, and news of the riot 'shocked the citizens of Grafton'. Business rivalry led in 1916 to the eventual replacement of Aldermen Strauss, Englert and Schaeffer from the Grafton City Council, but no one of German birth or extraction was interned at any stage of the war. Nor did this research reveal that anglicising of names occurred during or because of the war; the few such instances in the district dated to well before its outbreak.[28]

In his thesis on the German community in Bethania (Logan district), Raymond Holzheimer, descendant of one of the earliest settlers in the district, points out that 'the Bethania Germans appear to have escaped most of the disabilities of Germans in Australia during the war. There were no stories handed down of problems with officials or social disadvantages during the war'. His research further reveals that of the six men with German names who were discharged by Commissions of Peace for 'disloyal conduct', none came from the Logan district, and that the government did not remove the names of Germans from the list of Justices of the Peace as long as their loyalty remained unquestioned.[29] And John Cole, in his research into the Boonah shire, has this to say:

> By the turn of the century there still existed visible signs of a
> conscious desire to preserve aspects of German culture, but this was
> modified somewhat by the absence of a dogmatic adherence or
> allegiance to the fatherland. The Lutheran pastor who espoused the
> cause of Prussia during the early war years was quickly interned
> without evoking much sympathy in the local population.[30]

All of this supports Alan Corkhill's recent comment that 'despite the detention of controversial figures in the public sphere, the internment of Germans was kept to a minimum'.[31]

Down south in Tasmania, Marita Bardenhagen, in her work about the Germans during the Great War, also notes that no anglicising of names occurred because of the war.[32] More importantly, her assessment of 'conflict or unity' comes out firmly on the latter side: the Germans were loyal subjects, most young men faithfully joined up to fight for Australia and the Commonwealth, and none was disadvantaged because of his or her ancestry. The same goes for the large German communities in western and northern Victoria, and the even larger communities in the Albury, Walla Walla, Riverina and Germantown (Holbrook) regions of New South Wales. In Tumbarumba, a small town on the western outskirts of the Snowy Mountains, members of the German community were viciously attacked by fanatical anti-Germans in the local *Tumbarumba Times*,[33] but incidents like this in rural Australia, where four-fifth of the Germans lived, were the exception and not the rule.

In South Australia, country villages with a population of predominantly – if not exclusively – German origin, which allegedly had maintained their ancestral language and culture, are said to have been particular targets of suspicion when war broke out. This may have been the case but, as with the history of German rural communities in this state in general, more evidence is needed about what kind of harassment actually took place. On first sight it seems unlikely that the surveillance authorities would have squandered scant resources on remote settlements, and it is noteworthy that South Australia and Queensland, with the highest number of German settlers, had the lowest number of internees.

The bulk of people interned lived in the capital cities, and the reasons for this are not hard to find. In contrast to the majority of nineteen-century immigrants who settled in rural areas, and to whom German nationalism meant little, the later arrivals settled in the cities and were more prone to German patriotism. Moreover, memories of – and devotion to – their *Heimat* were still much fresher, making it more difficult for them that their old and new countries were at war. This contrast accounts for the fact that Western Australia, where large-scale German immigration only started with the discovery of gold in the 1890s, had a disproportionately high number of internees.[34] Yet even in the urban centres, the Germans who were directly affected were in a minority.

Consider the case of Fritz Müller, producer of mudguards and car radiators, which shows that some German-Australians benefited from the war. Having arrived as a 4-year-old in 1885, he set up a small soldering and car repair shop in Crown Street, Sydney a few years before the outbreak of war. After August 1914 Müller changed his name (and that of his company) to Frederick Muller, and he did such good business during the war that he was able to buy a much larger plant in 1919 on Parramatta Road, Camperdown and become Australia's major cooling-system manufacturer. Perusing the numerous biographies, like that of Paul Metzler for example, the reader is often scarcely aware that wartime measures were in place. And certainly there were voices among the Australian authorities who called for moderation. Arthur Griffith, Minister for Education in the New South Wales government, told his parliamentary colleagues in June 1915 that Australia was 'at war with the German nation . . . not with German literature'.[35]

It should also be noted that the Trading with the Enemy Act was primarily aimed to stop the export of lead, copper and zinc to Germany, which was Australia's chief customer for these minerals. That the imported material was used by the Reich for wartime purposes goes without saying. This explains the raid on the offices of BHP and other companies that had been trading with members of the Triple Alliance. Nor should we overlook the fact that the chief of German intelligence in the region, Walter de Haas, was the commercial attaché to the consulate-general in Sydney. His confidants included Oskar Plate, head of Norddeutscher Lloyd Steamship Company in Sydney, and prominent Sydney businessman Otto Bauer.

For most German-Australians, life went on as usual. At Hermannsburg, Pastor Carl Strehlow received the occasional visit from the authorities, who wanted to make sure that the missionaries were not indoctrinating Aborigines with German propaganda. To repel all doubts, Strehlow frequently played 'Rule Britannia' and other patriotic imperial songs on his gramophone. In only 6 of the 95 cases investigated by the Royal Commission into Property Holders of German Origin were acts of disloyalty found. In all other cases, the persons investigated were able to produce evidence from friends, neighbours or local dignitaries and officials attesting to their loyalty to Australia. Some had even contributed to the patriotic funds.

At around 25 000, the number of German Anzacs was high, and they fought well. They were drawn from the 5–6 per cent of the Australian population who were estimated to be of German descent shortly before the outbreak of war. Above all, there was John Monash,

Australia's most successful wartime general.[36] Corporal Edward Mattner became one of the most decorated men in the First Australian Imperial Force, and many others fought gallantly.[37] Sadly, while their sons were fighting at the front, there were cases of fathers being insulted at home because of their German background.

But in the end, verbal or written abuse, temporary dismissals of councillors or aldermen, threatening resolutions or the changing of German placenames cannot be ranked among the real tragedies of the war. These surely occurred elsewhere.

Historical presentation all too often suffers from a purely chronological approach, presented in white and black. With the outbreak of war the beautiful white of industrious German settlers adding vigorously to Australia's proud development turns into black, as cordiality gives way to harassment, malevolence and unjust, arbitrary internments. Such accounts make no allowance for the circumstances in which the stage was set: to that date, the most devastating and horrific war in human history. It is not true, as was portrayed in a soap opera screened on television in the late 1980s, that an Australian-German was bashed to death in an internment camp. Nor was there widespread torture of internees, as was claimed in a recent radio talk on SBS.[38] This is shoddy journalism and shoddy historical work that establishes little of value.

Inter-war years and World War II

The wounds left by World War I healed slowly. It is claimed at times that of all countries involved in the war, anti-Germanism was most pronounced and lasted longest in Australia.[39] This is a generalisation. Germanophobia was no less intense in most of the countries that had fought the Reich and sustained huge loss of human life and material damage, France above all. At the Versailles peace conference, the Australian prime minister, Billy Hughes, soon established himself as the number one German hater, surpassing everyone with his unrealistic demands for a 'Carthaginian Peace' for the 'Hun'. However, Hughes did manage to achieve Australian mandate over New Guinea, which had been a long-term strategic goal and offered promising economic prospects. Over 5000 Germans left Australia once peace had returned: 696 of them were deported and 4620 were listed as having departed voluntarily.

Officially, German immigration was banned until the end of 1925, as were German imports. In reality, the Australian authorities from the early 1920s permitted entry to German nationals in cases where families had been separated, or where there were other circumstances of personal hardship. The import ban, too, was lifted in August 1922. The former honorary consul for Brisbane, Eugen Hirschfeld, was permitted to settle in Australia again in 1926. On the other hand, all attempts by his family to allow Carl Zoeller to return failed. Before the war he owned a sugar mill in Baffle Creek, Queensland and, in the absence of his security file, it is idle to speculate why he was refused re-entry. Maybe it was the 'arbitrary and capricious' policies of the Australian authorities that accounted for their harsh stance;[40] on the other hand, given the fact that many others were allowed to return, there may well have been more to his case. Unable to return to his family, Zoeller committed suicide in Cape Town, South Africa, in November 1926.

For most, life gradually returned to normal. At Hermannsburg, shortly before his tragic death at Horseshoe Bend, Carl Strehlow had begun to wonder whether Europe's 'higher civilisation' was indeed the answer for the Aborigines. He now realised that the Europeans had robbed them of their most valuable possession – their land, the source of their life. On Strehlow's death his son, Theodor Strehlow, went to Adelaide to study, in preparation for a distinguished career as an anthropologist that was to extend over almost half a century. He gathered a vast and invaluable collection of sacred Aboriginal objects.

While Theodor Strehlow was preparing for his first major assignment with the Aborigines, Hans Heysen was painting pictures of amazing precision, catching the spirit of the Flinders Ranges as few others had. Heysen was born in Hamburg in 1877 and at the age of six his family emigrated to South Australia, where they settled in Adelaide. He showed an interest in painting from his early youth and soon embarked on an astonishingly successful career. With influential backers such as Dame Nellie Melba, Sir Lionel Lindsay and Sir Baldwin Spencer, Heysen staged several exhibitions, which further enhanced his reputation. When war came, neither he nor his family was harassed, but those years placed an enormous emotional strain on the young artist. Nevertheless, he soon regained his old enthusiasms. From 1926 onward he began to work in the Flinders Ranges, visiting the region frequently over the next few years. His output of sketches and watercolours, chiefly from the Aroona and Arkaba areas, was prolific. He was deeply in love with the Australian countryside and became one of the country's earliest conservationists.

Club life had also gradually restarted in all town and cities; the Concordia Club in Sydney, for example, regained its prewar membership of 300 by 1926. There had been no interruption to the teaching of German at the universities of Sydney and Melbourne during the war, and high schools soon began offering courses again. Most Lutheran churches had continued to conduct sermons in German throughout the war, provided they still had a pastor in command of the language, but the trend was to appoint Australian pastors who preached in English and by the end of the 1920s the process was virtually complete. Newspapers and publications such as club periodicals started to re-emerge, on the proviso that they not publish material detrimental to Australia. Most editors had no difficulty obliging, but the extreme right-wing, ardent German nationalist editor of the *Queensländer Herald*, Karl Reber, frequently got himself into trouble with his criticism of Australia and the postwar international arrangements. Diplomatic relations recommenced in 1924 with the reopening of the Consulate-General in Melbourne. The office was moved to Sydney in 1928 to be closer to Canberra, the new capital.

The first postwar consul-general, Hans Büsing, proved to be a competent administrator. Unlike his predecessors and his successor, Büsing was the only top diplomatic representative of the Reich who realised that *Deutschtum* had no basis and no future in Australia. He replaced *Deutschtumspolitik* with a more realistic concept, *Kulturpropaganda*, which simply aimed to convince the German-Australians to be just as proud of their homeland as British-Australians were of theirs. Against difficult odds, German–Australian trade relations improved steadily throughout the 1920s, and by 1929 German exports to Australia had recovered half their prewar market share. Thus, just as in Europe the Treaty of Locarno marked a brief period of international goodwill[41] and a ray of hope for a brighter peaceful future, in Australia, too, the animosity towards Germany (and Germans) was slowly ebbing.

When the cruiser *Berlin* visited Fremantle in 1928 on a goodwill tour, officers and men received a friendly welcome not only from the citizens of Perth but also from governmental officials and business people. This success encouraged the German navy in 1932 to dispatch another cruiser to call at Australian ports during a world tour. Again visits to Adelaide, Melbourne, Hobart and Sydney were well received. The German air ace Elly Beinhorn gained a great deal of attention when she called at Sydney in April 1932 on her solo flight around the world. By the early 1930s, normality was clearly returning.

Germans made news. Australians followed with fascination the search by Western Australian police, assisted by Aboriginal trackers,

Bertram and Klausemann with three of their rescuers: Maowl, Bilay and Constable Marshall

for two German pilots whose plane had crash-landed in the far north-west in May 1932. Hans Bertram and Adolf Klausemann had set out for Australia from Germany to promote their sturdy, reliable and versatile Junker W33, which had become famous for making the first east–west crossing of the North Atlantic. They had taken off from Koepang on the island of Timor on 15 May and run into a storm, which threw them 25 degrees off course. Lack of fuel forced them to land on remote Cape Berrima, out from Wyndham. They were found by an Aboriginal tracker on the brink of death forty days later. Their attempts to reach the outside world having failed, Klausemann had lost his sanity.

By the early 1930s a number of the Australian-German communities and organisations throughout southeastern Australia felt sufficiently confident to celebrate their half-century of existence. The handing over of the *Emden*'s nameplate by Prime Minister J. A. Lyons to the German consul-general at the beginning of 1933 symbolised the return of goodwill between the two countries. Meanwhile, in Adelaide a memorial of granite with a bronze plaque was erected in honour of Pastor August Kavel, leader of the first German immigrants to South Australia.

The 'seizure of power' by the Nazi Party on 31 January 1933 did not immediately impair the improving relations between Australia and Germany. The new regime seemed initially to bring some stability to the fatherland after the trouble-stricken, tumultuous years of the Weimar Republic and, as in many other countries, was tacitly supported by the Australian government and the bulk of the press (although the political left strongly condemned the Nazi system from the beginning). It did not take long, however, before the aggressive and militant foreign policies of Nazi Germany, coupled with the murderous policies pursued at home, confined support for the Hitler dictatorship to the lunatic fringe of the political right.

The Nazi organisation in Australia was small but very active. The first branches of the party were set up in Tanunda – on the initiative of Dr Johannes Becker, a medical practitioner who had arrived from Germany in 1927 to settle in the Barossa Valley – and in Sydney, where Johannes Frerck, a delicatessen owner, established a *Stützpunkt* [base] on 10 April 1934 at the Waratah Café in Kings Cross. Other branches soon followed in Adelaide, Melbourne and Sydney. Because both Becker and Frerck were fanatical Nazis, the new consul-general, Rudolf Asmis, had his own protégé, Walther Ladendorf, appointed to take over the main party office in Australia, as *Landkreisleiter* (district leader). Ladendorf's more subtle approach to spreading the Nazi gospel was seen as more effective in Australia. Asmis, who had replaced Hans Büsing in 1932, was a monarchist at heart like many of his superiors in the German Foreign Office, but like most members of that organisation he readily adapted to the new regime. Although he did not actually join the party until 1938, he industriously devoted himself to furthering its ends by means of 'peaceful penetration'.[42]

The most colourful personality in the Nazi organization, the editor of the local party newspaper *Die Brücke* (the bridge), Arno von Skerst, was not really a National Socialist but an opportunist adventurer with an amazing knack for taking the wrong step.[43] Of German Baltic nobility, von Skerst had worked for the Tsarist government, the White Russians, the Soviets, a Russian bank in Shanghai, a British-owned insurance company in Manchuria, the East China Railway Company and several international oil companies, before finally settling in 1933 in Sydney, where he was appointed first editor of *Die Brücke*, Dr Asmis's weekly newspaper in German and English. Asmis regarded the services of this most unusual yet very talented person to be a valuable asset in fostering Nazism in Australia.

Consul-General Rudolf Asmis speaking at a ceremony beside German war graves at Rookwood Cemetery in Sydney

For the next five years with *Die Brücke*, von Skerst intermingled Nazi propaganda with less spectacular news of local life in the numerous German communities throughout Australia. He also became secretary-general of the German-Australian Chamber of Commerce, one of whose functions was to ensure that only 'Aryan' firms were appointed as agents for German companies. As he was also the

*Running out of luck: Arno von Skerst and the Australian media (*Daily Telegraph, *29 August 1948)*

Australian representative of the German news agency, NDB, and for a time at least was Nazi *Schulungsleiter* (instruction leader), it is not surprising that von Skerst began to be noticed by the Australian security services. By the late 1930s he was variously described by military intelligence and others as 'a red hot Nazi and a big noise', 'a key Nazi', and the party's 'chief propagandist'. The security services were also convinced he was a German spy and, most probably, an agent of the Japanese Secret Service (on account of his many contacts with members of the Japanese community in Sydney).

Though the Nazi organisation never had more than 180 members, they were most active around the country, trying to convince people of the merits and achievements of National Socialism. They had no impact on the rural communities of German background, nor did their attempts to infiltrate the city clubs meet with much luck. Only in Sydney, because of the close proximity of the consulate-general, did they manage to gain some influence in the Concordia Club, but attempts to place the club fully under Nazi leadership failed. When war broke out the whole Nazi organisation was speedily arrested.

Larger numbers of Germans began to arrive again in Australia in the mid-1930s, but for altogether tragic reasons. To escape from the genocidal policies of the Hitler government approximately 8000 Jews, or people declared Jewish under the notorious Nazi Nuremberg Laws, make their way to Australia from Germany or Austria. The last 2000 of them arrived after the war had started, on the disreputable British troopship *Dunera*, and were interned with German nationals and prisoners of war, many of whom were ardent Nazis. The 'Dunera boys' had been sent to Australia as part of the British government's security measures, which included the deportation of thousands of internees, regarded as potential security risks, to Canada or Australia. After landing in Sydney and Melbourne they were removed to internment camps at Hay and Tatura. It took weeks, sometimes months, before the Australian authorities were made to understand why these young men had had to leave Nazi Germany – and ordered their release. Notwithstanding their harsh treatment, half of the 'Dunera boys' decided to stay in Australia after the war, and they made a valuable contribution to Australian society and culture.

Among the 7251 Germans interned (excluding the Jews) were 536 members of the Templer Society. A Pietist religious community that originated in Württemberg in 1861, the Templers moved to the Holy Land during the last quarter of the nineteenth century believing that here they would be closer to the spiritual temple of God. They too were deported to Australia by the British at the outbreak of war for security reasons. It is said, however, that 'internment in Australia was humane, giving the internees much self-administration'.[44] They also decided to stay in Australia after hostilities had ceased, and were soon joined by a further 700 of their brethren.

The statistics tell us that after World War II there were 14 567 German-born in Australia. Their number was soon to swell to unforeseen proportions.

7

WILLKOMMEN AGAIN

Political relations

For the Germans war was over on 8 May 1945; for the Australians it continued until 14 August. The creator of the Thousand-Year Empire, Adolf Hitler, had committed suicide five days before Germany's unconditional surrender, along with Eva Braun, whom he had married only a few days previously. Of the other Nazi leaders, Goebbels and his wife had also taken their lives just before the fall of Berlin, after poisoning their six small children. Many of the Nazi hierarchy, and also the rank and file, were either hiding in Germany to evade arrest or had already made plans to flee to remote regions such as South America, Australia or Africa. They had good reason to avoid facing justice. As the Allies closed in on Germany from both east and west they discovered evidence of indescribable barbarism. A few years of insane Nazi racialism had led to atrocities and bloodshed unparalleled in human history. Altogether, 50 million people had died as a result of Germany's quest for world power, and most of these were civilians who did not die in battle but were either murdered or had become casualties of total warfare. Many more millions were injured or crippled for life and an equally large number were made homeless. Germany, like most of Europe, lay in ruins.

Most cities and towns had been destroyed. Administrative, political and civilian institutions had broken down, along with food supplies and transport. Except for a few rural dwellers in the centre of the country, few Germans still lived in their homes. Millions had fled the urban areas to escape the Allied bombing raids; millions more had fled west before the advancing Red Army; and there were the beginnings of a movement in the other direction at the first appearance of Allied troops. Several million more non-German displaced persons had poured into Germany ahead of the advancing Red Army. Many were fleeing the battle zone, others fled because they were opposed to the emerging political and social system of the Soviet-dominated East, or because they had joined Hitler's anti-Bolshevik campaign and had good reason to fear reprisals. Now they were all lumped together in huge, speedily erected camps, many of which were located in Germany, to await their fate. Because of this, the history of the Germans in Australia soon took on new dimensions.

For Australia war lasted until the Japanese, too, surrendered unconditionally. This second world war came much closer to home, and there were raids on the Australian continent – although on a small scale compared with Europe. Nevertheless, the threat of the Japanese invasion forcefully demonstrated to Australians their strategic insecurity – a small community of predominantly white settlers so close to hundreds of millions of Asians. Most, regardless of their political opinion, wanted to keep Australia an Anglo-Celtic society, but the country's population growth had been very modest. And if Australia intended to continue its industrial growth, accelerated during the war, then measures had to be taken to overcome labour shortages. The chaotic conditions in Europe thus offered a chance to renew immigration on a scale not witnessed since the gold rush of a century earlier. At first it was hoped that the great majority of these new immigrants would come from the British Isles. But it soon became evident that their numbers would not meet the hoped-for annual intake (originally 70 000 per year). It was then that the Immigration Minister, Arthur Calwell, turned to the displaced people housed in Red Cross camps in Germany and other parts of Central Europe to fill the gap. This decision was to change Australia from a staunchly British society to one of the most tolerant multicultural societies of our time.

One of the ethnic groups soon to land and settle in Australia was the Germans. Inevitably, Australian–German relations were strained in the immediate postwar period, but in striking contrast to events after World War I, they improved surprisingly quickly. Signs that antagonism would be muted were already evident during deportation proceedings. Immediately after the war, 304 Germans were deported (241 men, 63 women, 24 children), comprising mainly German merchants and their families and a few Nazis – Johannes Becker, former party leader and longstanding member, among them. Maintaining that his life would be endangered back in Germany, Becker broke parole shortly before his scheduled departure and attempted to board a ship to South America. But he was arrested in Sydney and forced to leave Australia on the US army transport carrier *General Heintzelman* in December 1947. As far as most other Nazis were concerned the Australian authorities refrained from harsh action.

Oluf Bohlens, for example, had been deputy camp leader at Tatura and had a reputation among camp inmates as a staunch Nazi. The investigating officer, however, doubted this:

> He said he did not intend to be naturalised in 1939 because the war clouds were too heavy, leaving me with the impression that had it not been for the imminence of war he would have been naturalised. He is on friendly terms with an Australian woman whom he wants to marry, and was supporting a female illegitimate child born in Adelaide of another woman. I have to report that it is neither necessary nor advisable that he should be deported.[1]

Johannes Dietrich Cordes had served with the Brown Shirts (the *Sturm-Abteilung*, or Nazi storm-troopers) in Germany from 1933 to 1937 before he became a merchant seaman. His standing in the Nazi Party was sufficient to have him appointed head of Brown Shirt members on the *Aller*. He deserted the ship in an Australian port, which prompted the investigating officer to advise against deportation and instead support his application for permanent residence.

Karl Wilhelm Eidelback was described as a 'domineering old man'. Aged seventy-one at the time of his threatened deportation, he had been living in New Guinea for thirty years. Although he never joined the party he was, according to the investigating officer, 'very strongly pro-Nazi'. On the other hand:

> He has a de facto wife whom he described as a Filipino and whom the New Guinea administration claim was a Caroline Islander. By her he has two daughters. I think at his age he is harmless and is obviously genuinely fond of his family of whom he has heard recently. I do not find it necessary or advisable to report that he should be deported. There are difficulties in the way of him finding accommodation in Australia. Perhaps the matter may be submitted to the appropriate Minister for permission for him to join his family in New Guinea.[2]

Heinrich Flauaus had not been a member of the Nazi Party or any of its branches, but was interned for expressing pro-German views. In the opinion of the officer, however, this was brought about by his fellow workers at Mount Isa refusing to go down the mine with him, which was said to have left him 'a little embittered':[3]

> So the Australian authorities, in striking contrast to their behaviour in 1919, bent over backwards to refrain from deportation. Of the hundred or so Nazis interned at Tatura, only seven were finally recommended for further scrutiny and possible deportation. Even former leading Nazis in Australia managed to get permission to stay. Robert Julius Köhler, who had been the superintendent of the Hamburg-America Line in Australia and in charge of the Nazi labour front here, was originally singled out for deportation, but this, too, was later revoked on compassionate grounds. Köhler's appeal to be allowed to stay was assisted by his argument that he had left the Nazi organisation in 1939. In fact he had been asked to leave the Nazi Party because of his close association with Count von Luckner who, on his return to Germany from his world trip was put under Gestapo supervision because during the journey he had 'passed remarks about the party, not mentioned the Third Reich, not called upon its representatives nor respected them and . . . made pacifical speeches'.[4]

Even Arno von Skerst managed to avoid transportation, although his behaviour continued to be extremely erratic. He was among the first Germans interned at the outbreak of war. This was in part explained by his prominent role in the Nazi organisation, but also by close surveillance by Australia's military intelligence, who were certain that he was a German spy. They claimed to have 'reliable information' that von Skerst and other Nazis had been frequently seen aboard a motor vessel on Sydney Harbour, taking photographs with special cameras.

After the invasion of the Soviet Union by the *Wehrmacht* he changed course yet again, becoming a vociferous Soviet patriot. He also took on the role of a camp informer, compiling numerous reports on his former comrades. At the same time he wrote a series of letters to the Soviet Embassy in Canberra, asking for a Soviet passport. The letters were sprinkled with adulation for 'the talented leadership of Marshal Stalin', and on the 1943 anniversary of the October Revolution he sent the ambassador his 'sincerest congratulations'. Other letters to the Australian government praised the Allied victories in North Africa. Naturally, his change of heart was little appreciated, nor were his hopes for a positive response from the Soviet Embassy fulfilled. Some Australian officials favoured his early release, but he was kept at Tatura until March 1946.

Von Skerst's third marriage, in 1934, to the Australian manager of the corset department of Winn's store in Sydney, did not survive the stress of war. She divorced him after she herself was briefly interned in 1942. By the time he was allowed to leave Tatura he had achieved such notoriety that few of his prewar contacts cared to renew his acquaintance. His application for a position with the CSIRO was rejected on the grounds of security and fear of public reaction. With the assistance of the Quakers he became a servant for a wealthy Neutral Bay family. He later held a similar position at the King's School in Parramatta, which kept him going until 1948. In September that year newspaper interest and public outrage were revived when he was selected for a radio quiz program that was raising money for government loans. This brought calls for his deportation – which again he avoided, partly because he had married again, this time a woman many years his junior. It was this fourth marriage that finally broke his spirit. Left by his young wife, he turned on his gas oven and committed suicide. He had placed notes under his neighbours' doors apologising for the smell of gas.[5]

There are several reasons why Australian–German relations were less bitter this time. Direct military encounters between German and Australian troops were confined to North Africa, were of short duration and, in contrast to the horror of trench warfare, resulted in relatively few casualties. The Japanese became Australia's main enemy, and the atrocities committed against Australian soldiers and prisoners of war in South-East Asia, New Guinea and other islands overshadowed the news of Nazi crimes. In addition, when the defeat of the fascist powers was almost immediately followed by a sharp deterioration in relations between the Western Allies and the Soviet Union, Australians and most Germans found themselves in the same camp. In fact, Australian pilots participated in the Berlin airlift of 1948–49.

A goodwill tour by Pastor Martin Niemöller, president of the Evangelical Church in Hesse, across the Australian continent in 1949 also helped thaw relations. Organised by the World Council of Churches his visit showed that not all Germans had willingly supported the crimes of the Third Reich, and that many had suffered severely at the hands of the Nazis. And although the Australian media had given wide coverage to the horrific deeds committed by Nazi Germany, brought again to international attention by the Nuremberg Trials, a first postwar opinion poll conducted in 1948 about the desirability of immigrants put Germans second in popularity behind the British.[6]

Large-scale immigration of non-British migrants commenced in 1948. Preference was given to Eastern European refugees and to Italians, but a not-insignificant number of Germans gained entry.

Trade relations had re-emerged in a minor way by the late 1940s, and in January 1952 diplomatic relations with the Federal Republic of Germany (commonly referred to during the Cold War era as West Germany) were fully established, with a German ambassador appointed to Canberra and an Australian chargé d'affaires to Bonn.

The first visit by a senior Australian politician occurred in October 1953 when the foreign minister, Richard Casey, was received by President Theodor Heuss and Chancellor Konrad Adenauer. The atmosphere was most cordial and, at a dinner given by Adenauer in honour of his guest, the high quality German wine soon encouraged the two statesmen to sing Heinrich Heine's famous song 'The Loreley'. Casey had visited Germany as a student and had a good command of the German language. Impressed by their own performance, the duo then sang the old war song, 'Two Grenadiers Marched towards France'. The next day, the press mentioned only 'The Loreley'.[7]

Most amicable, too, was the visit of Prime Minister Robert Menzies to Germany in 1956. As Menzies was not interested in seeing factories or wartime damage, a special train took him via the romantic Rhine Valley to Heidelberg and the pretty medieval town of Rothenburg in Bavaria. In 1957 the German Foreign Minister Heinrich von Brentano visited Australia, where he was already confronted with concerns about the agricultural policies of the newly founded European Economic Community. Top-level visits between the two countries, however, remained few and far between. Gough Whitlam visited Bonn in 1975, President Walter Scheel toured Australia in 1978, as did Chancellor Helmut Kohl in 1988 and 1997, and President Richard von Weizsäcker in 1993. On the other hand, ministers and delegations from both countries visited each other regularly. Politically, harmony prevailed for the rest of the century, but on the economic level the sailing was not so smooth.

Diplomatic relations with the 'other' Germany, the German Democratic Republic (GDR), conventionally known as East Germany, were established by the Whitlam government in 1975, but political and economic intercourse between the two states remained insignificant.

Immigration

German immigration had begun well before the governments of the Federal Republic and Australia reached official agreement on the matter in 1952. Between 1947 and 1952, 240 experts in various fields were recruited by the Australian government under the Employment

Helmut Kohl (centre), then Premier of Rheinland-Pfalz and later Chancellor of the Federal Republic, visits a wildlife sanctuary near Canberra

of Scientific and Technical Enemy Aliens scheme for scientific projects and positions. A number of *Volksdeutsche* (Germans from outside the Reich who had been given the status of German citizens under the Nazis) gained entry as part of the Displaced Persons program, and they most likely included a fair number of Nazi war criminals. About 4600 Germans came to Australia over three years from 1949 to work on the Snowy Mountains project. Last but not least, the A. V. Jennings housing construction firm brought out 150 building tradesmen in 1951 to work in the rapidly expanding Australian capital. They became known as 'Jennings's Germans'.

News of government negotiations with the Federal Republic to include Germans in the assisted immigration scheme met with protests from the Australian Labor Party, sections of the trade union movement and members of the public at large, but Immigration Minister Harold Holt was undeterred. Opinion polls supported German immigration by a clear majority, and even the Returned Services League, fiercely anti-German after World War I, now backed the government's stance.[8] The agreement, signed in Bonn in August 1952, stipulated that the number of immigrants would be annually determined by mutual consultation. By 1954 the Census figures already listed the number of Germans at 65 422; they reached 109 315 in 1961, and 84 per cent were assisted migrants.[9] Just over 34 000 arrived between 1963 and 1973, but cheap airfares and the narrowing gap in living standards between the two countries led to a high return rate: approximately 30 per cent went back to Germany.

Decline in the Australian economy after the oil crisis of 1973 dramatically slowed this rate of immigration, to a net figure of 4770 in the 1970s.[10] This was followed by a sharp increase in the numbers seeking permanent entry visas – which it is claimed reached as many as 20 000 per annum – as the Cold War intensified in the late 1970s, due particularly to the arms race and the stationing of Pershing nuclear rockets on West German soil.[11]

But by now a change in Australian immigration policies brought about by the dawn of multiculturalism ensured that only a fraction of the applicants were successful: 2595 in both 1980/81 and 1981/82, and 4130 in 1982/83. On 1 January 1983 the government drastically cut the immigration intake, and German immigration since then has rarely exceeded 1000 per annum. All told, approximately 150 000 migrants came to Australia from the Federal Republic of Germany in the second half of the twentieth century. A little less than one-third returned. A further 50 000 German speakers immigrated from Austria, Switzerland and other parts of Europe and the Middle East.

Like their predecessors a century ago, the twentieth-century German immigrants adapted readily to Australian society and most did well for themselves. But unlike them, the great majority of German speakers (75 per cent) went to the big cities. Here they quickly assimilated. As the leading immigration expert, James Jupp, aptly comments, 'German immigrants settled into suburbia very quickly and quietly, becoming "invisible" by their conformity to established Australian norms'.[12] By the 1990s most German-born lived either in New South Wales (30 per cent) or in Victoria (27 per cent); the remainder went to Queensland (17.5 per cent), South Australia (12 per cent), Western Australia (9 per cent), the Australian Capital Territory and Tasmania (2 per cent each) and the Northern Territory (1 per cent). Ethnic and cultural similarities would have again accounted for the fact that

Germans, after the British, were continuously listed in opinion polls as the most popular immigrants and the most desirable neighbours. While skilled and semi-skilled migrants predominated at first, new immigration criteria meant that by the late 1970s German-speaking immigrants were often very well-to-do or came with special skills and experience. Their income distribution and education levels rank favourably compared to most other ethnic groups.[13]

One of the many results of the age of the computer is that writers can become their own publishers, and so the number of migrants telling us what it was like to settle in a new country far from their *Heimat* has greatly increased. Manuscripts that because of limited circulation potential were not attractive to established publishers can today be self-published at relatively low cost. One of the better of these books, *Einwandererschicksale*, not only makes for interesting reading but also provides valuable insight into the problems faced by migrants, the obstacles to be overcome, and the reasons for success (or lack thereof).

While most such stories fall into the successful category, there are of course exceptions.[14] Few could have been more unfortunate than Sigfried (Ziggy) Pohl. Coming home from work one day in 1973, Ziggy found his wife strangled on the floor of their house in Queanbeyan. He was charged with her murder, and in a scandalous miscarriage of justice was sentenced to life imprisonment on the basis of circumstantial evidence. He continued to protest his innocence, writing from gaol to countless institutions and politicians, including the then-president of the Federal Republic of Germany, Walter Scheel. It was all to no avail. Because of his exemplary behaviour Ziggy was released after ten years, his life in ruins. Seven years later, Roger Bawden, resident at the military academy in the Canberra suburb of Duntroon, went into the police station at Queanbeyan and confessed that he had killed Mrs Pohl. She had caught him red-handed after he had broken into the Pohls's house to steal valuables. It was two more years before Ziggy was granted an unconditional pardon; he was also awarded a huge indemnity. However, this would hardly have made up for the fact that twenty prime years of his life had been destroyed.

Trade and commerce

A delegation from the Federal Association of German Industries toured Australia in 1951 to look for new export markets, in the belief that the declining economic strength of the United Kingdom would leave a vacuum for West German businesses to fill. 'Germany had in the Australian market the unique opportunity', read their report, 'to move in as England did last century when Germans were struggling for unity and the foundation of the Reich'.[15] This was too optimistic an assessment, although history was to show that another former enemy country of Australia, namely Japan, did eventually replace Britain as the main trading partner. Still, German–Australian economic relations, after a difficult start, have remained solid ever since. The total value of goods exported to Germany in the first financial year after the war (1945/46) was £400. Imports from Germany fared little better, and in the 1945/46 and 1946/47 financial years only one piano was shipped to Australia. An increase of piano imports to six in 1948/49 shows that improvement was on the way, and trade figures quickly expanded after normality returned to Australian–West German diplomatic relations.

One of the first companies to establish itself down-under was Lurgi Chemical & Metallurgical Engineering, which converted brown coal into town gas that was then piped to Melbourne. Mercedes-Benz and Volkswagen arrived during the 1950s, the latter had already produced 100 000 'Beetles' by 1961. With the car industry came the subsidiary industries: the automotive electrical manufacturer Robert Bosch; the Hella company, which concentrates on production of car and truck lights, and the world-famous manufacturer of automotive instruments, VDO. The 1960s saw the arrival of Germany's chemical giants Bayer, BASF and Hoechst on the Australian scene, along with Lufthansa and the large ocean transport company Columbus Line. In the 1970s came some major mining and mine-equipment manufacturing industries, such as Ruhrkohle, Krupp, Mannesman and Thyssen, along with German banks and the electrical giant Siemens. The foundation of the German–Australian Trade Chamber in Sydney in 1977 gave further impetus, as did German–Australian business associations in Melbourne, Brisbane and Perth. By the early 1990s a number of German firms had more than 1000 employees.

Australian companies did not arrive in any significant way in Germany until the mid-1980s – when TNT, Australia's largest transport company, established TNT Deutschland, which was soon to employ a staff of 1800 people. Brambles Industries and the building materials company Boral, the second largest in the world, commenced business in the Federal Republic during the 1980s, and ANI (Australian National Industries), Burns Philp and the brewer Foster's followed in the early 1990s. The trade balance in the final decades of the twentieth century heavily favoured Germany. On average, Australia imported twice as much as it exported, and whereas Germany was Australia's ninth largest trading partner, Australia ranked thirty-fourth among the Federal Republic's partners.

This imbalance in trade was one source of concern (and complaint) from the Australian point of view, and the agricultural policies of the European Union was the other. Governments heavily subsidised the rural sector in most of continental Europe, which put the efficient (non-subsidised) Australian primary producers at a distinct trading disadvantage. The point was succinctly made in 1978 by Minister for Special Trade Relations in the Fraser government, R. V. Garland, who commented that a bovine flown to Frankfurt in a jumbo jet and fed champagne on the way was still cheaper than a European subsidised cow.[16]

Many German speakers who had settled in Australia established prosperous businesses. Bernard Hammerman, born in Berlin in 1913, came from a long line of fur traders and himself became an apprentice furrier at the age of fourteen. From his early youth he had had a keen interest in the arts and film-making and, with the fur industry suffering during the Great Depression, he worked for the German film company UFA as a cameraman. However, his hopes of eventually producing his own film were cut short in 1933 by the Nazis' seizure of power, which led immediately to acts of violence and discrimination against the Jewish community. When on return from his work at UFA one early summer morning that year Bernard witnessed the molestation of an elderly Jewish milkman by a group of young Nazi thugs, he came to the man's aid and soon put the assailants to flight; he was then forced to flee to England.

He arrived in London in August 1933, found employment with a British furrier company and learned English. In 1937 the Home Office refused to renew his permit to stay (unless he could set up a business employing British labour – out of the question in his case), but the Jewish Refugee Committee obtained a passage to New Zealand for him. When his ship docked at Sydney in March 1937 he decided to disembark, having received an offer of employment from David Jones.

From the beginning, Hammerman flourished in Australia. By 1941 he had set up his own fur business, which shortly before he died four decades later had grown to nine retail outlets around the country. The workroom in Sydney alone employed forty-two people. He was for many years the president of the Fur Traders Association. As a man of culture Hammerman worked tirelessly as a patron of the arts and to bring Australia closer to the 'New Australians' – as the postwar immigrants were called in the 1950s. In 1952 he was among the foundation members of the All Nations Club, an organisation that at its peak had 1400 members, and whose aim was to built a bridge between old and new Australians. According to Hammerman, many New Australians had no difficulties finding their way into business or religion in their new country, but they found it hard to make cultural contacts. The All Nations Club attempted to overcome this, and after initial difficulties the Guest of Honour list included such well-known people as Robert Morley, Barry Jones, Barry Humphries, Dr Frank Knopfelmacher, Sir Robert Menzies.

The All Nations Club had outlived its purpose by the 1970s, as the process of integrating the immigration community had largely been achieved, but in 1972 Bernard was appointed the first governor of the Power Foundation. Set up by the University of Sydney at the request of Dr John Power, who had bequeathed a large sum of money for the establishment of a fine arts centre, the foundation later became the Museum of Contemporary Arts. Hammerman was appointed because of his 'unique contribution' to Sydney's cultural life. He was also very active in the production of *The Bridge*, a magazine for the Jewish community. Not surprisingly, in 1982 Hammerman was awarded the Order of Australia for his services to the ethnic communities. Shortly after his seventieth birthday, on 21 April 1983, he collapsed and died in Amsterdam after attending the pre-eminent Frankfurt Fur Fair.

Harry Seidler was born and grew up in Vienna. When the *Anschluss* (the incorporation of Austria into Nazi Germany) came in 1938 Seidler's parents managed to get an entry visa for Australia, but Harry preferred to join his brother in Cambridge, where he attended the polytechnical school. In May 1940 both Harry and his brother were shipped as enemy aliens to Canada, where they spent seventeen months in internment. On release Harry studied architecture at the University of Manitoba, and in subsequent years was in contact with and greatly influenced by such leading exponents of modern European architecture as Walter Gropius and Marcel Breuer, who had been forced to move to North America during the 1930s. He was Breuer's chief assistant from 1946 to 1948, when he set up his own private practice in Sydney. Seidler's key role in post-1945 Australian architecture is evident: the Australia Square and MLC centre in Sydney, the Shell headquarters in Melbourne, the Riverside Centre in Brisbane, the Commonwealth Trade office complex in Canberra and the Australian Embassy in Paris are among his many architectural masterpieces.

One would expect Germans to feature prominently in Australia's current wine boom, and indeed German wine-growers are found in all major wine regions. Most famous, of course, is Wolf Blass. Blass learned the trade of a cellar master in the Rhine Hessia wine-growing area. In 1960 he came to Australia with little cash but equipped with the latest expertise in viticulture and plenty of energy. Twelve year later his red wines had won many medals and prizes, and today Wolf Blass wines are among the leaders in the Australian market.

Maintaining language and tradition

With the outbreak of war in 1939 all German clubs were closed again, to reopen once hostilities had ceased – as had been the case after World War I. The Allgemeiner Deutsche Verein in Adelaide had recommenced club life by 1947, little more than a year after the war in the Pacific ended. A year later the Tivoli Club in Melbourne followed suit, and by 1950 the Concordia Club in Sydney and the Deutscher Turnverein in Brisbane had also started to function again. The intake of German migrants in the 1950s meant that all the traditional clubs reached record membership levels. As their facilities could not cope with so many new members, people whose applications had been shelved set up their own organisations in the rapidly sprawling suburbs – for example, the German-Austrian community in Cabramatta in Sydney's west and the Teutonia Club in Melbourne's east. Many German clubs were founded in cities and towns where there had been none before, such as the Germania clubs in Newcastle and Wollongong, the Rhein-Donau Club in Perth and the German Harmonie Club in Canberra. By the end of the 1960s German clubs had also been established in Darwin and Hobart.

The aim of these organisations is basically the same: to provide a piece of the old *Heimat* in the new homeland. Here, homesick migrants can talk to people of their own background, play a game of *Skat* or skittles, and take part in such popular German festivities as the Oktoberfest or the Karnival. Thus maintenance of German tradition is central to all clubs' activities. The guidelines of the Rhein-Donau Club in Perth are typical: 'a small group of German speaking idealists have founded the club with the aim of conserving the German language, culture, customs and traditions, as well as for sociability and happy get-togethers and [so] add to the cultural life in Australia'. It seems that some clubs are concerned more with German language than with nationality. There are, for example, several German-Austrian communities in Sydney and one in Wodonga, and in Cairns we find the German-Austrian-Swiss Association.

A number of smaller societies perform a variety of functions. In her recent study of metropolitan Perth, Mary Meinecken-Cooley lists 13 German and German-speaking clubs, societies, associations and informal gatherings.[17] There is no consensus on their total number. The Department of Immigration and Ethnic Affairs recorded 83 German-speaking organisations throughout Australia in 1992,[18] but the fact that only four are listed for Western Australia suggests that the figure includes only larger bodies.

An umbrella organisation was founded in 1965, when 29 German clubs in Australia formed Die Brücke. This institution was originally designed for the provision of cheap group airfares to Europe, but its activities expanded into such fields as social assistance for members in need and exchange schemes for school students. The membership of Die Brücke in 1981 was 20 000. If allowance is made for non-German members, the figure seems to suggest that only 10–15 per cent of German speakers in Australia bother to join a German club. The majority obviously felt no desire or need to maintain closer links with their country of origin.

The ups and downs of German club life are well-illustrated by a brief look at the postwar history of the Concordia Club in Sydney – one of the oldest and largest in Australia. When the club reopened in the early 1950s the outlook seemed bleak. The secretary, Adolf Crausaz, merely hoped that the prewar membership of 274 would one day be regained. Of those 274, few were left: '55 have died, 20 have left the Club, another 20 have left the country, 30 have vanished without trace and the rest is sitting on the fence, waiting to see from which direction the wind will blow'.

He could not have been more wrong. The number of new members increased by twenty for each month of 1953. The Concordia Club's nightly dances were so popular that long queues were regular, and the list of membership applications was '*ellenlang*' (incredibly long). Membership stood at 600 by 1960 and rose to 1000 in 1962. Limited space meant that many applicants 'were so fobbed off that they would never be seen again'.[19] Enlargement of the facilities overcame this problem and membership peaked in 1969 at just under 4000. This success had its down-side: expansion gradually became the chief goal of the club's management and the big plans slowly loosened the roots of comradeship. While the skin of the club apple was becoming prettier, the inside was starting to rot – the euphoria of growth estranged members.[20]

Then came the changes to immigration policies. The number of Germans arriving in Australia began to dwindle, and from the 1980s onward the new arrivals were of a different type to those of the 1950s and 1960s. Most were well educated, had sufficient command of English and had left their home country for altogether different reasons. The old-fashioned atmosphere of the clubs had little appeal for them; nor did the sons and daughters of the postwar immigrants show much interest (and most descendants spoke no or little German). Membership began to decline, poker machines could not provide the sheet anchor and eventually, facing bankruptcy, the club had to sell its magnificent residence in Stanmore and settle for something far more modest.

Discussion of the Concordia Club should conclude with a brief reference to the poor fate of soccer in German-speaking Australia; even in the club's peak years the Concordia team made it only as far as the Sydney second division. And the situation in the other cities is no different. Today it is hard to find a club anywhere in Australia that has a large Austrian, German or Swiss membership. This is surprising given the huge popularity of the sport in the Federal Republic, and the fact that Germany, with Brazil, has the best international record in the history of the game. Partly it is explained again by the rapid integration and assimilation that marked German emigration to Australia from the beginning of European settlement. The Italian, Greek and Yugoslav communities were more supportive of club life and provided large crowds of spectators – hence clubs such as Apia or Pan Hellenic could afford the cost of semi-professionalism that characterised first-class soccer in Australia in the immediate postwar decades.

Concordia during the 1960s probably had enough income to back a premier team, but this was never seriously considered by the club management, who always maintained that the club's many sub-branches should all receive fair financial support. If anything, the club's soccer section was treated like Cinderella. And there is another reason for the lack of German success on Australian soccer fields. In the old country soccer has no competition. Here, many proud dads had to face the fact that because of peer-group pressure and media influence their talented, strong or tall *filius* had no interest in playing the 'world-game' and would rather join an Australian Rules or rugby team. Soccer in Australia has ranked among the also-rans as far as popularity is concerned and is virtually restricted to postwar immigrant groups.

Most German-speaking organisations were social clubs, but of course other associations and communities were not without importance. Attention should be drawn, in particular, to the welfare societies that arose in some cities in the wake of the mass migration of the 1950 and 1960s.

Irmhild Beinssen was born in 1910 at Elberfeld (in the Rhineland) and later moved to Berlin for her secondary education. In January 1933 she met her husband-to-be, Ekkehard Beinssen, an Australian of German origin. The two were soon forced to leave Germany for political reasons – they had fallen foul of the Gestapo – and lived for the next five years in California. They then decided to move to Australia, where Ekkehard joined his father's wool business. No sooner had they arrived than Australia found itself at war with Germany, which brought difficult years for the couple and their children. They were temporarily interned before a legal friend secured their release in 1944. After the war they moved to Sydney, where they participated in the rebuilding of the German Evangelical-Lutheran Church community. They also played a leading role in the Occupied Europe Relief Society, which sent food and clothes to Germany. In 1954 Irmhild Beinssen became the president of the Australian-German Welfare Society, which had been founded by Johanna Hess, wife of the first West German ambassador to Australia, and a small circle of German women:

> She brought with her qualifications that weighed far more than her organisational talent: she knew the German colony of pre-war days, the people who had been interned, German-speaking immigrants from various countries. Above all she knew their problems, for had she not herself had to start from scratch several times? She spoke good English and, by reading the books that her sister, a student of Social Studies at Sydney University, had to read, was able to prepare herself theoretically for the task. Added to all this was the attraction of a challenge.[21]

As president for over thirty years, Irmhild Beinssen gave invaluable service to the community. In Melbourne, journalist Ruth Isle set up a similar organisation, and there was also a German-Australian Welfare Association in Perth.

On the cultural level a number of Goethe societies provided meeting places and extensive German libraries for those seeking intellectual stimulation. Goethe Institutes, as the Federal Republic's cultural institutes are officially called, were set up in Melbourne (1972) and in Sydney and Canberra (1974), primarily to stimulate and promote German-language teaching; but they also organise conferences, guest lectures, musical performances and art shows. The closure of the

Goethe Society in Canberra in 1998 is perhaps an early sign that the vibrant role of German-speaking people in Australia's modern history may be waning.

Saturday schools have also contributed to the teaching of the German language. These were set up in the 1950s and 1960s because of pressure from German parents who wanted to encourage the use of German outside the immediate family. This it was hoped would ensure that their children did not forget the German language. Initially, these Saturday schools relied completely on voluntary private funding because the assimilationist policies of the Australian government at that time did not give much encouragement to such ethnocentric tendencies. But with the arrival of multicultural Australia in the 1980s and 1990s, these schools received government funding and language teaching was encouraged at the primary level. German was also taught widely in secondary schools, both state and private, and at universities. With the expansion of the tertiary sector, the number of German departments rose from two in 1965 to eleven in 1975. Of the many successful teachers of German language and literature, Wuppertal-born Richard Herbert Samuel, Professor of German at the University of Melbourne (1951–69), has often been praised for his services to the community. Appointed to succeed Augustin Lodewyckx, he maintained his predecessor's fine scholarly tradition and raised the discipline to international standards.[22]

Cultural contributions

Cultural relations commenced in the mid-1950s when both the Alexander von Humboldt Foundation and the German Academic Exchange Service offered research and postgraduate scholarships to Australian students and academics. The establishment of Goethe Institutes in Melbourne, Sydney and Canberra in the 1970s by the Federal Republic marked the beginning of a substantial academic give-and-take in the humanities. Since then cultural programs, language courses, co-operation between universities, workshops on literature and language, the staging of art, music, theatre and film events and festivals have flourished. The list of Australian orchestras touring West German cities and vice versa is extensive, as is the list of art exhibitions mounted in the two countries.[23] The German contribution to the 1988 bicentennial celebration was substantial; most notable to the general public was the *Gorch Fock* in the tall ships regatta and Richard Wagner's *Meistersinger* at the Sydney Opera House.[24]

Cultural contacts with the GDR remained low key, as had political and economic relations. Nevertheless, a number of unionists, academics and others participated in the Australia–GDR Friendship Society, which maintained links with the League of Friendship in East Berlin. Among other things this meant that in the final years of the Cold War, marked by the Gorbachev thaw, East German artists could tour Australia. The GDR Ballet gave performances in most capital cities, as did some orchestras and the Berlin Ensemble's leading Bertold Brecht actor, Ekkehard Schall. During the bicentenary a descendant of Ludwig Leichhardt, also called Ludwig, whose physical features – to the amazement of the Sydney media – bore a striking resemblance to the explorer's, attended a conference on Australian exploration held at the University of New South Wales. His visit opened up links with Leichhardt circles in the explorer's home country, the Cottbus district of Brandenburg where, led by local historian Helmut Donner and in virtual international isolation, an enormous amount of work had been produced about Leichhardt, his family, friends and supporters.

The genocidal policies of Nazi Germany ensured that, as in the nineteenth century, the German contribution to music was large. Of the many conductors, composers, singers, instrumentalists and other professional musicians who ended up here in their escape from Nazi violence, Richard Goldner should be mentioned first. A Jewish refugee, he arrived from Vienna in 1939, having been the principal violinist and violist of the Simon Pullman Chamber Orchestra and the Hermann Scherchen Musica Viva Symphony. After the war he formed Richard Goldner's Sydney Musica Viva, a seventeen-piece orchestra that developed into the Musica Viva Society of Australia, the principal chamber network and one of the foremost concert-giving organisations in the country. Goldner was supported by two keen (and prosperous) musicologists, Alfred Wenkart, also from Austria, and Walter Dullo, who had fled Germany. Curt Prerauer had established a reputation in Germany as a pianist, conductor (at the Berlin State Opera) and composer before becoming one of Australia's most respected music journalists. Three more music critics had fled the old continent: Felix Werder, Hans Forst and Eva Wagner.

So too did conductors Henry Krips, Kurt Herweg and Georg Tintner. Krips had performed at the Burger Theater and Volksoper in Vienna, and became conductor of the Adelaide Symphony Orchestra after the war. He was known in particular as 'the man who brought Mahler to Australia'.[25] Tintner, who had been assistant conductor at the Vienna Volksoper, joined the national opera company in 1954 as conductor and later worked for the Elizabethan Opera Trust, and pioneered opera on ABC television. Stefan Haag was stranded in Melbourne in 1939 when touring with the Vienna Boys' Choir. He became principal singer with the National Theatre Opera Trust Company, and his 1949 production of *The Tales of Hoffman* had a lasting impact. This was only the beginning. Haag was production director then executive director for the Elizabethan Trust Opera from 1956 to 1969 – then 'This complete man of the theatre, singer, director, producer, lighting and set designer'[26] worked for the Tivoli, Sydney's new cabaret-restaurant, promoted successful productions such as *Hair* and *Jesus Christ Superstar*, introduced a half-price ticket scheme, promoted Aboriginal theatre, and even staged a disco-dance group in Cairns. And another fine musician, Stephan Ammer from Freiburg near the Black Forest, worked for many years for the Elder Conservatorium at the University of Adelaide.

Of the long list of German composers, lack of space permits me to include only the most successful and well known. George Dreyfus was born in 1928 in Wuppertal and came to Australia with his family ten years later. He completed a diploma of music at the University of Melbourne's conservatorium and became a bassoonist, first at Her Majesty's Theatre (1948–62) and then with the Melbourne Symphony Orchestra (1953–64). His success at composition allowed him to take this up full-time in 1965. His first opera, *Garni Sands*, written in 1961, was performed in Sydney, Melbourne and New York. In the early 1960s he wrote the score for two television series, *Australian Painters* and *Sebastian the Fox*, and his theme for *Rush* (1974) became a popular hit, selling 35 000 copies. Dreyfus's first symphony was composed in 1967 and his Sextet for Didjeridu and Wind Instruments (1971) is ranked as a landmark in modern Australian music.

During a long involvement with Melbourne's legendary Pram Factory, Dreyfus wrote the music for several plays, including Graham Blundell's *The Sentimental Bloke*; *Charles Rasp*, a ballad for choir and concert band about the German co-founder of BHP and, last but not least, *Manning Clark's History of Australia: The Musical*. In the 1990s he turned to European themes in his operas, creating *Rathenau* in 1992 and *The Marx Sisters* in 1995. Staged in Kassel in 1993, *Rathenau* was the first opera by an Australian composer to receive a German premiere. It deals with Walther Rathenau, a leading German-Jewish industrialist and the foreign minister of the Weimar Republic, whose assassination in 1920 was the first major act in the looming anti-Semitic murder campaign of the Nazi Party. The opera has been compared to Dreyfus's own family life; his father, who came to Australia unwillingly, died here unable to adopt his new home in favour of the Germany he loved.[27]

One of Australia's best-known sculptors, Bert Flügelman, arrived from Vienna in 1938. He studied art at the East Sydney Technical College and then went to the United Kingdom, Europe and the United States. He returned to Sydney in 1956 to teach art at his former college and at the University of Sydney and the newly founded University of New South Wales. From 1973 he taught for two decades at the South Australian Art School. Of his large number of sculptures in stainless steel, often using geometric forms or tubular shapes, *The Festival Sculpture* in Adelaide is probably best known. Other noted German-speaking sculptors are John Alisher and Ann Graham, both from Vienna, who arrived in 1935, and Inge King and Eleanore Lang.

Ludwig Hirschfeld-Mack was one of the 'Dunera boys'. He was born in 1893 at Frankfurt, the son of Ernst, a leather goods manufacturer and his wife Clara, née Mack, both members of the Evangelical Church. Ludwig showed an interest in art from an early age, and studied painting and crafts at Munich. He fought with the German army in World War I and was awarded the Iron Cross. After the war he joined the Bauhaus in Weimar, the avant-garde of the German art movement, where he studied under such painters as Paul Klee and Wassily Kandinsky; his chief teacher, Lyonel Feininger, was in charge of the print shop. Hirschfeld-Mack was interested above all in the application of colour theories and built an apparatus that combined moving projections of coloured light, mechanical templates and music of his own composition. He gained considerable fame with an explanatory booklet on the topic and gave performances in Berlin, Vienna and Leipzig. When designated Jewish under the Nuremberg Racial Laws, he left for England in 1936 and was deported to Australia in 1940 as an enemy alien. After two years in internment camps in New South Wales and Victoria (which he made the subject of a number of woodcuts), he was released through the sponsorship of James Darling, headmaster of Geelong Grammar School, and was appointed art master there. He taught his students the Bauhaus principles of self-knowledge, economy of material and form, and reform of society through art. He continued to teach and exhibit until his death in 1965.[28]

Sali Herman was of Swiss-Jewish origin. The eleventh of nineteen children, he came to Australia in 1937 with his wife and two children for fear of being blacklisted by Nazi sympathisers (his mother had emigrated after World War I with some of the smaller children because one of her brothers was already living in Melbourne). In Melbourne he joined the George Bell studio and became an official war artist. After the war he became famous for his paintings of Sydney. He captured the texture of the outside walls of weathered houses, with human figures, animals and birds adding a quiet sense of old suburbia. The best known of his paintings is perhaps *Potts Point* (1957), in which, under a milky sky, a woman feeds cats beside bleached terrace houses on the harbour's edge.[29] Herman continued painting well into his nineties. A self-portrait at the age of ninety-two shows him in his garden feeding the birds and animals against a backdrop of subtropical nature.

Hans Heysen's daughter Nora was the only one of his eight children who took to painting. Following in her father's footsteps she became noted for flower paintings and portraits, and won the Archibald Prize for portraiture in 1938. She, too, was an official war artist. Wolfgang Gresse is a leading representative of the Vienna School of modern fantasy art. He came to Australia in the late 1960s to overcome his *Angst* – the fear of war and terror. At the age of fifteen he saw the burning of Dresden, and after the war a Soviet court in the eastern zone of Germany sentenced him to eight years' imprisonment for political subversion. His powerful works concentrate upon the nuclear apocalypse that many in the 1970s and 1980s feared was imminent. Mention should also be made of world-famous photographer Helmut Newton, another refugee from Nazism.

The German Literature Archive in Marburg was surprised to receive a letter in 1965, posted in Melbourne, from Paul Hatvani, one of Europe's leading expressionist writers who had been lost sight of for over three decades. Born in 1982 in Vienna, Paul Hirsch began to write under the pseudonym Paul Hatvani while still at school in Budapest. He later made a career as a chemist, although he continued to publish extensively and was credited by the archive with over eighty published works on the theme of German expressionism. He arrived in Melbourne shortly before the outbreak of war, and it was not until after his retirement in 1965 that he resumed contact with the world of letters. In the remaining ten years of his life he published a further twenty-one texts, mainly in Germany, but he became known in Australia for an essay entitled 'Neither Here nor There'. Stephen Jeffries sums up the spirit of that essay, which is familiar to many newcomers:

Having come as a refugee [Hirsch] felt that he had 'an unresolved fate' in Europe and that he himself could never become a completely integrated Australian. Yet at this point, and this testifies to his strength of character, he does not bemoan a sense of loss . . . Rather, he bears witness to the process whereby German-speaking immigrants to Australia helped their new host society to expand and become industrialised. For Hirsch and subsequent generations of German-speaking settlers Australia was a place they wished to see profit from the advanced knowledge and sophisticated industrial techniques that they brought with them.[30]

In retrospect, Hirsch was pleased that the efforts of his generation had helped to overcome Australia's colonial outlook. By the 1960s Victoria was no longer only mercantile and agrarian in orientation. Hirsch, who had worked in the chemical industry in Melbourne, states clearly that he was proud to have helped Australia to industrialise. He had early recognised a real need for skills such as his and, like so many people educated in German-speaking countries, he brought to Australia a thorough scientific training and a fundamental belief in the ability of the educated mind to order things and events rationally.[31]

Gerhard Schulz, who taught German at university in Australia for many years, is probably the most prolific published writer in German. He was honoured by being mentioned in the autobiography of the famous German literary critic, Marcel Reich-Ranicki, as a very good stylist. Four German-speaking poets, Margret Diesendorf, Walter Billeter, Rudi Krausmann and Manfred Jurgensen, have recently attracted international attention, though little in Australian literary circles. Introducing Austrian-born Krausmann, the writer and critic Walter Tonetto is impressed not only with his poetry:

The restlessness of dégagé and ennuyé Krausmann, his sense of alienation from a Europe that is not the Europe of his youth – perhaps it never was – and from a thowless Australia that could never quite become as linguistically playful and culturally enticing a place as Austrian culture has been for centuries, result in a curiously divided existence.[32]

Jurgensen's home country is Schleswig, a mixed Danish-German community that had traditionally belonged to Denmark but became one of the first victims of Bismarckian power politics when in 1864 it was incorporated into Prussia. Jurgensen arrived in Melbourne in 1961, studied Arts at the University of Melbourne, and became acquainted with leading intellectuals, including Vincent Buckley and Germaine Greer. 'Picture him during his teenaged, Teddy-boyish days', writes Tonetto, 'a snivelly bosthoon, temulent and intemperate, plimsolled and sporting on occasion a pique devant, Vandyke beard, and an *accroche-coeur*, even in those early years he is a thoroughgoing rake, with a distinct Catalinarian, iracondulous air, to judge by the photos of the day'.[33] As Professor of German at the University of Queensland, Jurgensen has actively followed the footsteps of Augustin Lodewyckx and Richard Samuel in maintaining and strengthening the teaching of German language, literature and culture 'down under'.

EPILOGUE

The rise of multiculturalism

The aim of the postwar immigration program was to keep Australia white, to make the nation strong enough to maintain its European tradition in a world of Asian neighbours. But as it soon turned out, the chances of these plans succeeding were slim. Initially, the key word for the mass intake of migrants from Europe was 'assimilation': it was expected that the New Australians would readily adapt to their adopted country. Migrants were encouraged to convert quickly to Australian citizenship, with all its rights and duties. Assimilation was successful, and newcomers from northern Europe, the Dutch, Germans and Scandinavians, did indeed integrate readily and were largely accepted by the Australian population. On the other hand, assimilation was more difficult for the southern European migrants, in particular Italians and Greeks. They were the largest migrant groups in the 1950s and 1960s, and they were far less prepared to give up their traditional customs, habits and languages.

Paradoxically, the assimilation policy carried the germs of its own destruction. Because the New Australians were entitled after naturalisation to full citizenship, they could soon participate in and add their weight to the formation of new guidelines for Australia's future. Assimilation was politically successful, but a failure on social and cultural levels, and hence was abandoned in 1964.[1] Talk about the need for 'integration' lingered for a few more years, but the writing was clearly on the wall and immigration policies were to face fundamental changes.

It had become clear by the end of the 1960s that not only were the days of (official) assimilation and integration policies numbered, but also that the concept of White Australia itself was under challenge – soon to be finished altogether. The chief political parties (Liberal, Country and Labor) deleted this principle – the very key to Australian immigration since the turn of the century – from their programs in 1965.

Public opinion, however, lagged well behind the politicians. Large sections of the community were only just beginning to realise that the Australia of the future would be a very different one from that of their fathers. The goodwill of the first postwar years, which in the Cold War era offered a relatively friendly welcome to immigrants who had been forced to flee their homelands by the 'Russians' and the 'Communists', now gave way to reservation and xenophobia. Expressions like 'reffo' and 'bloody Balts' left little doubt about how many Australians viewed the non-British arrivals. But even the word 'Poms', for immigrants from England – normally a harmless term for British opponents in international cricket and rugby games – was heard increasingly outside this context. Discrimination against new arrivals was commonplace, and the mass immigration from Asian countries that marked the 1980s and 1990s would have been unthinkable.

The favourable economic climate of the 1960s encouraged a change of attitude, as did a general increase in the standard of education, the many positive experiences with the newcomers, the numerous achievements migrants brought to culture, sport and gastronomy, and the mere fact that people were getting used to one another. Vast improvements in communication, in particular the introduction of satellite television, connected the continent ever more closely to the outside world. Then there was the global condemnation of ethnic and racial discrimination. The Human Rights resolutions of the United Nations isolated states that pursued racialist policies, finally excluding these countries from the community of nations altogether (note the sanctions against the Republic of South Africa).

In Australia things did not get that far. A plebiscite held in 1967 gave a clear mandate to the government to give full citizenship to the Aboriginal people. By the end of the 1960s an increasing number of 'distinguished non-Europeans' were beginning to enter Australia. By the early 1970s economic factors added their weight again. The United Kingdom's entry to the European Community (later the European Union) weakened its commitment to the British Commonwealth; at the same time, East and South-East Asia were becoming economically more important for Australia. Initially, it was above all Japan that played a leading role in Australian economic policies, and soon became the country's main trading partner. Thus it was only a matter of time before the first Labor government since 1949, that of Gough Whitlam, officially abandoned the White Australia policy immediately upon taking up office in 1972: Australian immigration policies would no longer discriminate on the basis of race or colour. The first major wave of Asian immigration occurred in the late 1970s, when the Fraser government granted asylum to 90 000 Indochinese refugees. In the 1980s and 1990s the majority of immigrants came from non-European countries. Australia now began to see itself as a multinational community.

German prospects and retrospects

The intake of Germans was drastically affected by this shift from Europe to Asia. The number of German immigrants through most of the 1970s was small; indeed it barely surpassed the number of those returning to Germany.[2] It peaked again briefly in the late 1970s and early 1980s due to escalation of the Cold War, fear of nuclear confrontation and concerns about Europe's declining environment. More than 20 000 applications per annum are said to have reached the Australian embassy in Bonn in the early 1980s, of which only one in ten succeeded.[3] Aside from the fact that images of a nuclear-safe, environmentally clean country 'down-under' were largely illusory, the Australian government, keen to improve industry and modernise the economic sector in general, was not interested in people who wanted more or less to 'drop out'. Assisted immigration was halted altogether in 1982, and as Australia became ever more integrated into the Asia-Pacific economic region, immigration from Asia is now more lucrative than from Europe. Allowance is still made for political refugees, and a substantial number of people fleeing the war-torn remnants of the former Yugoslavia came during the 1990s.

The number of new German arrivals with permanent resident status over the last ten years has remained at just under 1000 per annum. Most come for professional reasons (specialists attracted by well-paid employment) or personal reasons (marriage), and a few may settle here to enjoy a warmer climate. This annual intake is just enough to maintain the level of German-born citizens at around 110 000, where it has stood since 1971. But as Australia's overall population has greatly increased, the German share is getting smaller every year.

This trend is unlikely to change, as neither 'pull' nor 'push' factors are likely to encourage a return to large-scale German immigration. Economically, Australia is doing well as part of APEC (Asia Pacific Economic Co-operation); politically, Australian relations with some Asian countries, in particular the Muslim states of Malaysia and Indonesia, are not as cordial – but this does not cause much headache to most Australian politicians. Nor is the situation in Germany conducive to renewed large-scale emigration. Few Germans would come to Australia today to escape the threat of political violence.

They would be coming to the wrong place in any case. September 11 and other terrorist attacks have illustrated that warfare is taking new directions. While the Howard government is the most vociferous supporter of President Bush's War on Terror and war in Iraq, attacks are more likely to occur in Australia than in Germany, where political opinion is almost unanimously opposed to the US policies. The nightclubs selected by Muslim extremists for the 'Bali bombing' were frequented predominantly by Australians.

Nor are people likely nowadays to leave Germany for Australia in order to escape pollution and damage to nature. Australia's environmental policies do not rank high internationally. Together with the United States, the Australian government is the firmest opponent of the Kyoto protocol aimed at reducing carbon dioxide emissions, which are held largely responsible for the current global warming. By far the driest continent in any case, two hundred years of European settlement have wreaked enormous damage not only on the Indigenous population but also on Australia's fauna and flora. Vast parts of Western Australia, South Australia, Victoria and New South Wales have for years been in an almost permanent state of drought, and scarce resources are gobbled up by the extensive cultivation of cotton and rice, plants that require huge amounts of water. At the same time, inland country towns are constantly on the verge of running out of drinking water. There are no effective plans to tackle this ever-deteriorating situation. In the country's tropical north, massive floodwaters drain into the ocean every year. Of course, it would be very expensive to channel this water to the south, where it is badly needed, and desalination would be similarly costly. Yet, as billions of dollars are spent to support the dubious US Middle East policies, it seems strange that there are few funds for more important, indeed vital, projects. The influence of the Green Party in Germany, on the other hand, has led to a marked improvement there. The gloomy and grey industrial centres of former days are gone, air pollution is low, and the forests have recovered from acid rain.

So, most likely the number of German-born citizens in Australia will dwindle, as have the Baltic communities and Czechs, Poles and Hungarians. Yet history is known to take strange courses, contemporary history in particular. No one predicted the fall of the Berlin Wall and the sudden collapse of the Soviet Empire – nor the events of September 11. A renewed 'push-pull' scenario is unlikely, but cannot be ruled out altogether.

A few years ago, the member for the federal seat of Oxley, Pauline Hanson, in her maiden speech to parliament demanded a radical change to Australia's domestic and foreign policies: immigration from Asia and other non-European countries should be stopped, social 'handouts' to the Aboriginal people should be greatly reduced, protective tariffs for primary and secondary industries should be restored and the country should pull out of the global economy. Hanson then left the Liberal Party to found her own One Nation Party. Political ineptitude and infighting led to that party's relatively speedy demise – but not before it handed out a few shocks to the established parties at state and local elections. Australia's strong economic position rules out a turn to political radicalism at present, but economies are known to go in circles. A serious decline in living conditions might lead to a right-wing backlash, a call to stop Asian and other 'coloured' immigration and, instead, to 'pull' in Europeans again.

And Germans might be 'pushed' to go. German re-unification was implemented largely at the expense of the East German workforce, leaving many people in the New Federal States permanently unemployed. Nowadays, the West German workforce is the hardest hit by the recent eastward expansion of the European Union. Companies employ 'cheap' Polish labour or move their plants and factories east, where production costs can be kept lower. Unemployment in Germany at the time of writing is around 4.5 million, bringing back memories of the Great Depression that brought in the Nazis. The generous German welfare state is crumbling, the social security net is being eroded. Should Australia call again by offering a better life, as happened in the past, then there might be another big wave of German emigration.

But doubtful as the future of the German communities in Australia may be, the past is certainly flourishing. In the 2001 Census, over 700 000 Australians stated that they had German ancestry – a surprising increase of 100 000 over the 1996 figure. Obviously it is popular to have a German background. Family histories are published in large numbers, as are biographies, and *Ahnenforschung* (genealogy) generally is flourishing.

The Paechs have one of the longest and proudest traditions. Among the first wave of Lutheran settlers to arrive in the nineteenth century, their influence in Tanunda was so important that part of the township was soon called Paechtown. Family members held important positions in South Australian society – from parliament to the business world, and Paechs were found in all walks of life. Other branches went to Victoria and New South Wales, where again they did well. Their long list of achievements includes the renowned Paech Bakery in New South Wales.

In the 1990s Alison Paech went back to the country the first Paechs had left. She lived in Warsaw from 1991 to 2001 and, accompanied by her father Allister Paech, traced the family's ancestry. Rentschein in the Züllichau district of the former Prussian Province of Silesia had become part of Poland. The German population had been expelled after the victorious Allies redrew the maps of Europe to rule out renewed German aggression. Her ancestors' home village, Rentschein, was now called Radoszyn and there was no more trace of the Paechs. As elsewhere in the district, tombstones had been removed, graves vandalised and headstones used to build houses. In Züllichau (now called Sulechow), some of the buildings from Prussian times were still standing, although in a dilapidated state, and she could locate the point on the River Oder where the Old Lutherans had departed in 1838. The local historian was critical of interpretations that ascribed religious motives to the Lutheran emigration of the late 1830s, and prefered an economic explanation. Obviously this Polish scholar had been trained in the Marxist tradition, which gives little credit to non-economic factors in the shaping of history. A family chronicle lists almost 1000 Paech family members throughout southeastern Australia.

Christian and Anna Elizabeth Rüdiger, also from Prussia's River Oder country, set sail for Australia with four of their children on the *Emmy* in August 1849. The majority of the 400 passengers had been signed up by agent Delius, and hence were heading for Melbourne. Sadly, Christian Rüdiger died on board only days before the *Emmy* reached Port Phillip, and was buried at sea. Anna Elizabeth with her children and other relatives continued on to Port Adelaide, and settled in the German village of Rosenthal (Rosedale). This was the beginning of a large family tree pieced together by two industrious family genealogists a century and a quarter later.[4] Today the number of descendants of Christian and Anna, mainly from South Australia and Victoria, is close to 2000.[5]

The same goes for the Waldeck family, whose ancestors, Friedrick Waldeck and his wife Friederika Wilhelmina, were the first German settlers in the Swan River colony. The couple arrived in 1836, initially to conduct mission work among Aborigines in the Perth region. They soon abandoned those plans and instead opened a tailoring and drapery business – though their son Christian was later supervisor of the Methodist Sunday School and superintendent of a missionary farm in Wanneroo called the Natives' Experimental Farm, where he was in charge of Aboriginal children's schooling and Bible study. Eventually the tailoring business so prospered that the Waldecks were able to purchase a large property at Greenough, where they lived until their deaths – which for both arrived at a very old age. The couple had eleven children, of whom most continued their parents' active participation in the Methodist Church. In 1979 the Reverend G. L. Waldeck produced a family tree that listed the 11 children, 75 grandchildren and 206 great-grandchildren – around 2000 persons related to the original Waldecks. Today Waldecks garden centres are a household name in Perth and so are Waldeck wines.[6]

Bernd Hüppauff arrived at the University of New South Wales in the late 1970s to take up an appointment in the School of German. He was surprised to find that many Hüppauffs had made their way to Australia long before. Ernst Wilhelm Hüppauff, again from Silesia, and his wife had settled in the Old Lutheran community of Bethany in South Australia in 1850, and some of their children and grandchildren had moved to Western Australia at the end of the nineteenth century. At a family reunion in Tanunda in 1984, Bernd compiled a 200-page family tree of the Hüppauff family.

Maintaining German tradition is again popular in Australia. At the University of Adelaide, Lee Kersten, who teaches in the Centre for European Studies, takes her students for a walk around town to show them that there is evidence of the German past everywhere. In the parks on the northern side of the Torrens River is the site of the school where missionaries Schürmann and Teichelmann taught the children of the local Aboriginal tribe (the Kaurna) in the late 1830s and early 1840s. The parklands themselves were designed by another German, August Pelzer.

Many people of German origin had connections to the old and new Parliament Houses in North Terrace, and in Government House, further up the road, Conrad Laucke was lieutenant-governor for a number of years. Former South Australian premier, Donald Dunstan, came from a family that changed its name from Kallosche to Dunstan during World War I. The University of Adelaide claims many prominent Germans and there are valuable German manuscripts in the State Library. Many of the artefacts collected by father and son Strehlow are displayed in the South Australian Museum, paintings by Australian-German artists hang in the Art Gallery, and Richard Schomburgk, Maurice Holtzer and Baron von Mueller helped establish the Adelaide Botanic Garden. Around the corner in Rundle Street East was Kindermann's Café, and in Hindmarsh Square there used to be a German pub, the Black Eagle. Lord mayors Bartels and Tiedemann once occupied the Town Hall in King William Street, and many Germans worked in the Education Department in Flinders Street. Menz Biscuit Factory, the biggest confectioner in Adelaide, used to be in Wakefield Street, and in the same street lived descendants of Carl Linger, composer of the state's anthem, 'Song of Australia'.

In the city square mile there are many Lutheran churches and offices, and at the Central Market in Grote Street, Barossa butchers and bakers offer a large variety of German food: *Bienenstich* and *Streusel* cake, *Mettwurst* and *Lachsschinken*, dill gherkins and sauerkraut. During World War I, an attempt was made to change the name of the most popular German sausage from Pork Fritz to Pork Austral. This failed, but *Berliners* (German-style donuts filled with jam) became Kitchener buns.[7]

In Queensland, the other state with a strong German tradition, five councils along the Leichhardt Highway (Dalby, Wambo, Chinchilla, Murilla and Taroom) staged a spectacular five-day Leichhardt Expo in September 2004, 'Food, Fun, Facts and Friends':

> delegates, many from Brisbane, tour through five council areas in the Western Downs for the fast moving program comprising 15 meals and cuppas, including a prize-winning sausage breakfast, 25 guest speakers and presenters from the UK, Germany, US, Darwin, Perth, Adelaide, Hobart, Melbourne, Sydney and Brisbane, plus four MPs, all contained within 17 major points of interest along the Leichhardt track.[8]

Germany's foremost Leichhardt scholar, Bernd Marx, and leading University of Melbourne authority on German explorers and scientists, Professor Rod Home, gave keynote addresses, and a local poet added some inspiring verse:

Sugared Tea and slabs of Fatcake, lazy lizards for each meal;
Strips of salted beef and honey, could you get a better deal?
'Use the Land' was Leichhardt's motto, like the natives in that part
Who in history's feeble contest, plunged a spear through Gilbert's heart.

Prince of Explorers, where you rest we cannot yet deliver
Though the trees are marked with 'L' along the Maranoa River.
Your mystery lies scattered now, the answers have departed,
And your destiny, unlike those tracks, remains today un-charted.[9]

Well received as the event was in Australia – the ABC's Colin Munro
was there from beginning to end – the Leichhardt Expo generated no
interest in Germany. Though well advertised, no enquiries for tickets were received in Leichhardt's home country. Nor would German
newspapers in Australia provide any coverage without advertising support, which was bewildering to the organisers. They could only conclude that Australians of German descent were totally unaware of the
Leichhardt Legend.

Assessing the German contribution

How then is one to assess the German contribution to Australian
history? This is not easy. The English, as James Jupp has recently
pointed out again, have given Australia its political, legal and administrative systems: government based on a lower house majority and
collective responsibility through a Cabinet from parties commanding
a majority in this house; a legal system that accepts English prece-
dents, including those predating the establishment of the Commonwealth of Australia; an electoral system based on distinct geographical
constituencies; and a public service and judiciary that are assumed to
be willing to serve alternating governments without prejudice.[10]

The Irish have been credited with playing an important part in
the formation of the labour movement, and noted historian of the
Irish in Australia, Patrick O'Farrell, commented once that Irish good
nature and unshakeable humour added a degree of light-heartedness
to Australian society, accounting for the easy-going attitudes 'down-
under'. Such observations are of course hard to prove (and if they can
be substantiated, then Professor O'Farrell certainly would have been
an exception to the rule). But there is no major asset of Australian
society today that can be traced back exclusively to the influence of the
German settlers. The German contribution was solid. They were the
third-largest group of European settlers in nineteenth-century South

Australia and Queensland, the fourth-largest in Australia as a whole before World War I, the fifth-largest in the immigration period after World War II, the sixth-largest ethnic group in Australia today, and on the statistics go.

If we look at prominent people today, we note German ancestry in all walks of life. Tim Fischer, leader of the National Party (1990–99) and deputy prime minister (1996–99) comes from the nineteenth-century German community in the Albury region of New South Wales. On the opposite side of the political spectrum the family of Meredith Burgmann, president of the New South Wales Legislative Council and grand lady of the New South Wales Labor Party left, goes back to German coopers who settled around Taree in the 1870s. Her uncle, Ernest Henry Burgmann, Anglican Bishop for Canberra and Goulburn, became famous for his biting social criticisms and greatly antagonised the political establishment by becoming the president of the Australia-Soviet Friendship League in World War II. The ancestry of leading Sydney legal firm, Clayton Utz, goes back to John Frederick Utz, who established the Sunlight Flower Mill at Glen Innes in 1881 and was mayor of the municipality in 1883. Sir Gustav Nossal, president of the Australian Academy of Sciences (1994–98), director of the Walter and Eliza Hall Institute in Melbourne, member of the World Health Organisation and recipient of many international awards and honorary degrees, was the child of pre-World War II Austrian refugees. And so was John Richard Pilger, one of the most severe international critics of US global policies, most recently the US invasion of Iraq.

Then there are the sporting heroes. One of Queensland's top crick-eters, Carl Rackemann, regarded by some sports commentators as having been one of the fastest bowlers in Australia, has German ancestry. The same goes for leading South Australian batsman Daryl Lehmann; and Carl Ditterich, ruckman in the 1966 St Kilda team – the only one to win the premiership for the Saints – had German parents. In Rugby League, speedy Queensland and Australian half-back Allan Langer is of German origin, and the ancestors of New South Wales full-back Andrew Ettinghausen were among the first group to settle in the Shoalhaven region in the 1850s. One would expect German and Austrian soccer players to feature prominently – and indeed, Leopold Baumgartner (born in Vienna, 1932), Manfred Schaeffer (born in Königsberg, East Prussia, 1943) and Les Scheinpflug (born Yugoslav *Volksdeutsche*, 1938) figure prominently in the Who's Who of Australian soccer. Yet no German team ever managed to play among the top teams in its state (in its heyday the most successful one, Concordia, only made it to the Sydney second division).

And this brings us back to why it is so difficult to find something pointedly German in Australia – the Germans assimilated too readily into the Australian lifestyle. Whereas Italians, Greeks and Chinese, and later Vietnamese, Turks and many others, managed to put their stamp on metropolitan suburbs – Germans did not do this. Mediterranean, Hungarian, Polish and Czech clubs rallied behind their teams financially and in terms of spectator support. The Concordia Club, on the other hand, treated its soccer section like the proverbial stepdaughter. There are no German equivalents of the distinctly Italian restaurants in Melbourne's Lygon Street, Carlton, or in Sydney's Norton Street, Leichhardt; there is no German equivalent to Chinatown. And though we find Indian, Vietnamese and Japanese food outlets in every suburb, places offering German cuisine are few and far between. Only the Oktoberfest is celebrated widely in many cities and towns, and not only in October – German *Feste* modelled on the Munich original are held throughout the year. Accompanied by the proper oom-pa-pa music, Bavarian beer and various tasty *Würste* and *Brezel*, they provide lots of fun for big crowds. So maybe the observation of a noted scholar more than thirty years ago – that the lasting additions of German culture to Australia were the Christmas tree, cake, sausages and sauerkraut – holds true after all.[11] But then these are important contributions. Aren't they?

NOTES

Introduction

1 Jupp, 'The Hidden Migrants: German-Speakers in Australia Since 1950', pp. 63–4.
2 Castles, Kalantzis and Cope, *Ethnic Conflict and Social Cohesion*, pp. 1–8; Tampke, 'Die multikulturelle Gesellschaft der Gegenwart', p. 115.

1 Why do people migrate?

1 Bade, *Auswanderer-Wanderarbeiter-Gastarbeiter*, p. 125.
2 Tipton, *A History of Germany since 1815*, p. 42.
3 Ibid., pp. 31–3.
4 Walker, *Germany and the Emigration 1816–1885*, pp. 162–3.
5 The northern states of Oldenburg and Hanover joined later, and so did the Hanseatic cities. The Austrian Empire remained outside the *Zollverein*.
6 Walker, *Germany and the Emigration 1816–1885*, pp. 54–5.
7 Ibid., p. 166.
8 Ibid., p. 167.
9 Bade, *Auswanderer-Wanderarbeiter-Gastarbeiter*, pp. 262–3.
10 Jupp, *The English in Australia*, p. 69.
11 New South Wales Legislative Council, Foreign Immigration, 14 September 1859, cited in R. Holzheimer, The Bethania Germans, MA thesis, University of New England, 2003, p. 16.
12 W. Kirchner, *Australien und seine Vortheile für Auswanderer*, Frankfurt (Main), H. L. Brunner, 1848; translated in Cloos and Tampke (eds), *'Greetings from the Land where Milk and Honey Flows'*, pp. 51–85.
13 S. Jeffries, 'German Settlement in Eastern Australia', in J. Jupp (ed.), *The Australian People: An Encyclopedia of the Nation, Its People and Their Origins*, Sydney, Angus and Robertson, 1988, p. 484.

14 P. Kneipp, 'The Ursuline Order in Armidale', in Voigt, *New Beginnings*, pp. 188–98.
15 S. Castles and M. Miller, *The Age of Migration: International Population Movements in the Modern World*, London, Macmillan, 1993, pp. 19ff.
16 F. Lüthke, *Psychologie der Auswanderung*, Weinheim, Studienverlag, 1989, cited in R. Barth, Deutsche Einwanderung in Australien seit 1945, MA thesis, Universität Tübingen, 1996, pp. 39–41.

2 The first fifty years

1 P. A. Johnson, 'Augustus Alt: The Life of Australia's First Surveyor-General to 1788', *Journal of the Royal Australian Historical Society*, vol. 74, no. 1, 1988, pp. 11–21.
2 Harmstorf and Cigler, *The Germans in Australia*, p. 5.
3 Von Stieglitz moved to Ireland in 1802, but after the death of the baron in 1824 the family faced destitution and decided to emigrate to Van Diemen's Land. See *Australian Dictionary of Biography*, vol. 2, Melbourne, Melbourne University Press, 1967, pp. 556–7.
4 Harmstorf and Cigler, *The Germans in Australia*, pp. 5–6; Mennicken-Coley, *The Germans in Western Australia*, p. 16.
5 Hudtwalcker to James Colqhoun, 2 Jan. 1835, Australian Agricultural Company, Deposit no. 160/923, Archives of Business and Labour, Australian National University.
6 Ibid.
7 Ibid., Minutes of Committee of Management, Australian Agricultural Company, 6 Feb. 1835.
8 'Untersuchungsakten betreff Transport von Strafgefangenen nach der englischen Kolonie Neu-Süd Wales', Staatsarchiv Hamburg, 331–2, Polizeibehörde – Kriminal, Jahrgang 1835, no. 1809 I.
9 Edward Macarthur to R. E. Jones, 29 August 1836, Mitchell Library A 284 (Petitions to the King, 1835–37).
10 Cloos and Tampke (eds), '*Greetings from the Land where Milk and Honey Flows*', pp. 11–12.
11 William Macarthur, *The Culture of the Vine, Fermentation and the Management of the Wine in the Cellar*, Camden, 1844, pp. iv–v.
12 Clark, 'Confessional Policy and the Limits of State Action', p. 992.
13 Cited in Voigt, *Australien und Deutschland*, p. 19.
14 J. M. Ey, *Mittheilungen über die Auswanderung der preussichen Lutheraner nach Südaustralien sowie über die Entstehung und Entwicklung der australisch-lutherischen Kirche*, Adelaide, Verlag der Druckerei des Lutherischen Kirchenboten, 1880, pp. 43–4.
15 Ibid., p. 18.
16 W. Iwan, *Um des Glaubens Willen nach Australien: Eine Episode deutscher Auswanderung*, Breslau, Verlag des Lutherischen Büchervereins, 1931, p. 28.

17 Walker, *Germany and the Emigration 1816–1885*, pp. 78–9.
18 A. Kavel, *Berichte deutscher Auswanderer in Süd-Australien*, Bremen, G. Hunkel, 1845, pp. 14–16.
19 Harmstorf, 'German Settlement in South Australia until 1914', p. 362.

3 Scientists and explorers

1 Cited in Tampke and Doxford, *Australia Willkommen*, p. 8.
2 Voigt, *New Beginnings*, p. 13.
3 Clark, 'Charles von Hügel', p. 4.
4 Quoted in Mennicken-Coley, *The Germans in Western Australia*, p. 3.
5 Clark, 'Charles von Hügel', p. 14.
6 These have been translated by Dymphna Clark in Clark (ed.), *New Holland Journal*.
7 Cited in Voigt, *New Beginnings*, p. 54.
8 Lodewyckx, *Die Deutschen in Australien*, p. 77.
9 Tampke and Doxford, *Australia Willkommen*, pp. 39–42.
10 Aurousseau, *The Letters of F. W. Ludwig Leichhardt*, vol. 3, p. 839.
11 Sprod, 'Leichhardt's Second Expedition 1846–1847'.
12 Aurousseau, *The Letters of F. W. Ludwig Leichhardt*, vol. 3, p. 104.
13 Traces found suggest that Adolph Classen may have been the only survivor of the expedition. For a stimulating account, see B. Marx, 'Die Suche nach der verschollenen 3. Leichhardt Expedition', in 'Ludwig Leichhardt', *Natur und Landschaft in der Niederlausitz*, vol. 19, pp. 149–81.
14 Tampke and Doxford, *Australia Willkommen*, p. 49.
15 B. Marx, 'Die Suche nach der verschollenen 3. Leichhardt Expedition', in 'Ludwig Leichardt', *Natur und Landschaft in der Niederlausitz*, vol. 19, pp. 6–22.
16 Tipping (ed.), *Ludwig Becker*, pp. 25–6; Tampke and Doxford, *Australia Willkommen*, pp. 50–2.
17 A. Buhl, 'Baron Ferdinand von Müller: A German Botanist in Australia', in H. Lamping and M. Linke (eds), 'Australia: Studies on the History of Discovery and Exploration', *Frankfurter Wirtschafts und Sozialgeographische Schriften*, vol. 65, p. 81.
18 Kynaston, *A Man on the Edge*, p. 323.
19 Mennicken-Coley, *The Germans in Western Australia*, pp. 3–5.
20 Cited in Tampke and Doxford, *Australia Willkommen*, p. 53.
21 *Australian Dictionary of Biography*, vol. 5, Melbourne, Melbourne University Press, 1974, pp. 42–4.
22 D. Sandemann, 'Robert von Lendenfeld: Biologist, Alpinist and Scholar', in Tampke and Walker, *From Berlin to the Burdekin*, pp. 67–80; the order was later reversed and the higher peak was named Mt Kosciusko.

23 T. G. Vallance, 'Early German Connections with Natural History, Geology and Mining in New South Wales and Queensland', in Voigt, *New Beginnings*, pp. 269–78.

24 Sumner, *A Woman in the Wilderness*.

4 Missionaries

1 *Kirchen – und Missions-Zeitung*, vol. 47, 1911, p. 175.

2 H. J. J. Sparks, *Queensland's First Free Settlers 1838–1938*, Brisbane, Queensland's First Free Settlers Centenary Committee, 1938.

3 M. Linke, 'Geographical Observations of the Bohemian and Moravian Brothers in Australia', in H. Lamping and M. Linke (eds), 'Australia. Studies on the History of Discovery and Exploration', *Frankfurter Wirtschafts und Sozialgeographische Schriften*, vol. 65, 1994, pp. 19–32.

4 Darragh and Wuchatsch, *From Hamburg to Hobsons Bay*, pp. 140–2.

5 G. Hacchius, *Hannoversche Missionsgeschichte*, Hermannsburg, Druck und Verlag der Missionshandlung, 1907, vol. 2, pp. 16–17.

6 Ibid., vol. 3, pp. 48–9.

7 Ibid., vol. 3, p. 50.

8 *Hermannsburge Missionsblatt*, vol. 14, 1867, p. 68.

9 Ibid., vol. 16, 1869, p. 98.

10 M. Hartwig, Progress of White Settlement in the Alice Springs District c.1860–1894, PhD thesis, University of Adelaide, 1970, pp. 459–79.

11 Hacchius, *Hannoversche Missionsgeschichte*, vol. 3, pp. 353–5.

12 Hartwig, Progress of White Settlement in the Alice Springs District, p. 546.

13 J. Flierl, *Forty-Five Years in New Guinea*, Columbus OH, Board of Foreign Missions of the Evangelical Lutheran Synod of Iowa and Other States, 1925 pp. 20–1.

14 P. Scherer, 'Looking Back', *Lutheran Herald*, vol. 46, 8 October 1966, pp. 304–5.

15 Reuther to Deinzer (Neuendettelsau), 17 June 1906; Reuther to Kaibel, 11 July 1906, 14 Jan. 1907; Kaibel to Reuther, 11 April 1906, 31 May 1906; Kaibel to Mr Ch. De Pierre, 10 Oct. 1906 (Lutheran Archive, Adelaide).

16 Note his 'Sagen und Sittender Dieri Stämme in Zentral-Australien', *Globus*, Jan. 1910.

17 Veit, 'In Search of Carl Strehlow', pp. 108–34.

18 Durack, *The Rock in the Sand*, pp. 46–7.

5 The golden age

1 The often cited figure of 55 000, based on Mönckmeier's work of 1912, is far too low (W. Mönkmeier, *Die deutsche Überseeische Auswanderung*, Jena, Fischer, 1912). It does not include the pre-1847 immigrants, the

sizeable number who left from non-German ports and the gold-seekers from California, and completely leaves out emigration to Tasmania and Western Australia.

2 Harmstorf, 'German Settlement in South Australia until 1914', pp. 360–1.
3 Ibid., p. 361.
4 E. Gohl and R. Vollmer (eds), 'Death of Mr. Louis Ballhausen' in Die Reise von Clausthal am Harz nach Süd Australien: Die zwei Tagebücher des Louis Ballhausen, manuscript, State Library of New South Wales, pp. iii–iv.
5 Cloos and Tampke (eds), 'Greetings from the Land Where Milk and Honey Flows', pp. 14–16.
6 Cited in Darragh and Wuchatsch, From Hamburg to Hobsons Bay, p. 1.
7 Ibid., pp. 2–3.
8 For details about the controversy surrounding Westgarth's migrants, see ibid., pp. 37–52; C. Meyer, A History of the Germans in Australia 1839–1945, Melbourne, Monash University, 1990.
9 Bardenhagen, Lilydale, p. 9.
10 Voigt, Australien und Deutschland, p. 36; Cloos and Tampke (eds), 'Greetings from the Land Where Milk and Honey Flows', pp. 17–18; G. Burckhardt and Mackay, History of the German Community in the Clarence River District of NSW, pp. 18–19, 34–6; R. Holzheimer, The Bethania Germans, MA thesis, University of New England, 2003, p. 15.
11 Burckhardt and Mackay, History of the German Community in the Clarence River District of NSW, pp. 13–17.
12 Cloos and Tampke (eds), 'Greetings from the Land Where Milk and Honey Flows', p. 18.
13 Two children between 4 and 14 counted as an adult: adult meant above 14 (Holzheimer, The Bethania Germans, p. 20).
14 J. C. Heussler, Kurze Beschreibung der Kolonie Queensland, Frankfurt, Franz Benjamin Auffahrt, p. 34.
15 Tampke and Doxford, Australia Willkommen, p. 107.
16 Holzheimer, The Bethania Germans, p. 22.
17 His own claim to have brought out 6000 immigrants from Germany probably puts the figure too high.
18 D. Nagel, 'Johann Christian Heussler: A Father of Queensland', in Voigt, New Beginnings, 122–9.
19 For details and history of subsequent legislation, see Holzheimer, The Bethania Germans, pp. 24–9.
20 C. Meyer, A History of the Germans in Australia 1839–1945, Melbourne, Monash University, 1990, p. 47.
21 Harmstorf and Cigler, The Germans in Australia, p. 34.
22 Meyer, A History of the Germans in Australia 1839–1945, pp. 68–9.
23 Tampke and Doxford, Australia Willkommen, pp. 121–2.
24 Meyer, A History of the Germans in Australia 1839–1945, p. 47.

25 J. Cole, 'Farm and Family in Boonah', in Voigt, *New Beginnings*, p. 87.
26 Holzheimer, The Bethania Germans, p. 58.
27 It is not possible to estimate the number of Germans on the goldfields. While 10 481 were listed in Victoria in 1861, there are no comparative figures for New South Wales and Queensland.
28 Petersen, *Zur Situation des Deutschen als Fremdsprache im multikulturellen Australien*, p. 24.
29 Voigt, Australien und Deutschland, p. 25.
30 Tampke and Doxford, *Australia Willkommen*, pp. 113–14.
31 Mennicken-Coley, *The Germans in Western Australia*, pp. 29–44.
32 Williams, *German Anzacs and the First World War*, p. 19.
33 Harmstorf, 'German Settlement in South Australia Until 1914', p. 364.
34 Voigt, Australien und Deutschland, pp. 32–3.
35 Mennicken-Coley, *The Germans in Western Australia*, pp. 37–8.
36 M. Tipping, 'Ludwig Becker and Eugène von Guérard: German Artists and the Aboriginal Habitat', in Tampke and Walker, *From Berlin to the Burdekin*, pp. 81–107.
37 McCredie, 'German Musical Tradition in South Australia', pp. 60–1.
38 Ibid., p. 61.
39 C. Robson, 'The Germans in Queensland', in Harmstorf and Schwerdtfeger, *The German Experience of Australia 1833–1938*, p. 107.
40 See pp. 111–16.
41 I. Harmstorf in *Australian Dictionary of Biography*, vol. 7, Melbourne, Melbourne University Press, 1979, p. 240.
42 Corkhill, 'The German Language Press in Australia and the Mechanics of Survival', p. 310.

6   The shadow years

1 R. J. Evans, *The Coming of the Third Reich*, Allen Lane, 2003, pp. 8–9.
2 C. Clark, *Kaiser Wilhelm II*, Harlow, Longman, 2000, p. 4.
3 Designed by the Chief of the German General Staff in 1905, the plan was to quickly overrun France by invasion from the north, then concentrate on defeating the Tsarist Empire. This meant advancing through Belgium and Luxembourg, and hence violating Belgium neutrality, and was certain to bring the British Empire into the war.
4 F. Fischer, *Germany's War Aims in the First World War*, New York, Norton and Co., 1967, pp. 95–119.
5 R. C. Thompson, *Australian Imperialism in the Pacific: The Expansionist Era, 1820–1920*, Melbourne, Melbourne University Press, 1980, p. 65.
6 Tampke (ed.), *'Ruthless Warfare'*.
7 A. Brooking, 'A Foreign and Trade Policy Perspective on the Australia–German Partnership', in Jurgensen, *German–Australian Cultural Relations since 1945*, p. 21.

8 Cited in J. H. Voigt, 'The German National Festival in Sydney before World War I', in Voigt, *New Beginnings*, p. 142.

9 Ibid., p. 144.

10 J. A. Moses, '"Deutschtumspolitik" in Australia: From Kaiserreich to Third Reich', in Harmstorf and Schwerdtfeger, *The German Experience of Australia 1833–1938*, p. 127.

11 J. Priest, 'The Thiess Role in Australian Development', in Voigt, *New Beginnings*, p. 105.

12 R. Webster and A. Miller, *First Class Cricket in Australia*, Melbourne, self-published, 1991.

13 Harmstorf, 'German Settlement in South Australia until 1914', p. 363.

14 Ibid., p. 362.

15 J. A. Moses, *Australia and the Kaiser's War*, Brisbane, Broughton Press, 1993, p. 10.

16 Moses, '"Deutschtumspolitik"', p. 127.

17 S. Macintyre, *The Oxford History of Australia*, vol. 4, *1901–1942: The Succeeding Age*, Melbourne, Oxford University Press, 1986, p. 147.

18 On the appalling record of German war atrocities, see J. Horn and A. Kramer, *German Atrocities 1914: A History of Denial*, London, Yale University Press, 2001.

19 Quoted in M. McKernan, *The Australian People and the Great War*, Melbourne, Nelson, 1980.

20 Cited in M. McKernan, *The Australian People and the Great War*, Melbourne, Thomas Nelson, 1980, p. 165.

21 Mennicken-Coley, *The Germans in Western Australia*, p. 52.

22 G. Fischer, *Enemy Aliens: Internment and the Homefront Experience in Australia 191–1920*, Brisbane, Queensland University Press, 1990, pp. 108–9.

23 Mennicken-Coley, *The Germans in Western Australia*, p. 49.

24 J. Clark, *Dr. Maximilian Herz. Surgeon Extraordinaire: The Human Price of Civil and Medical Bigotry in Australia*, Sydney, self-publication, 1976.

25 Voigt, *Australien und Deutschland*, p. 118.

26 R. Davies, Some Aspects of the Government's Response to the Presence of Germans and German Descendants in Australia 1914–1918, PhD thesis, University of Melbourne, 1981, p. 8.

27 Tampke (ed.), *'Ruthless Warfare'*, p. 28.

28 Burckhardt and Mackay, *History of the German Community in the Clarence River District of NSW*, pp. 83–9.

29 R. Holzheimer, The Bethania Germans, MA thesis, University of New England, 2003, pp. 129–30.

30 J. Cole, 'Farm and Family in Boonah 1870–1914: An Ethnic Perspective', in Voigt, *New Beginnings*, p. 91.

31 Corkhill, 'German Settlement in Queensland 1838–1939, p. 369.

32 Bardenhagen, Lilydale, p. 59.

33 Williams, *German Anzacs and the First World War*, pp. 179–200.

34 Mennicken-Coley, *The Germans in Western Australia*, p. 65.

35 Voigt, New Beginnings, p. 117.

36 Williams, *German Anzacs and the First World War*, pp. 5–8.

37 Ibid., p. 159 and passim.

38 'Internment of Germans during World War One', SBS Radio, 16 Sept. 2004.

39 J. Perkins, Germans in Australia during the First World War, in J. Jupp, *The Australian People*, Melbourne, Cambridge University Press, 2001, p. 40.

40 G. Fischer, *Enemy Aliens*, p. 120.

41 Signed by the Foreign Ministers of Germany (Gustav Stresemann), Great Britain (Sir Austen Chamberlain) and France (Aristide Briand), the Locarno treaty set out to return goodwill and normality to Western Europe. It was disavowed by the Hitler government in 1933.

42 On the Nazis in Australia, see J. Perkins, 'The Swastika Down Under: Nazi Activities in Australia, 1933–1939', *Journal of Contemporary History*, vol. 25, no. 1, 1991, pp. 111–29; 'The Struggle for Control of Hitler's Nazi Party in Australia in the 1930s', *Journal of the Royal Australian Historical Society*, vol. 82, no. 1, 1996, pp. 88–105; 'An Old-Style Imperialist as National Socialist: Consul General Dr Rudolf Asmis (1879–1945?)', in J. Milfull (ed.), *The Attractions of Fascism*, New York / Oxford, Berg, 1990, pp. 291–306; 'Johannes Heinrich Becker: Medical Practitioner and Nazi', *Australian Dictionary of Biography*, vol. 13, Melbourne, Melbourne University Press, 1993, p. 148.

43 J. Perkins, 'Arnold von Skerst: Nazi Propagandist', *Australian Dictionary of Biography*, vol. 11, Melbourne, Melbourne University Press, 1988, p. 621.

44 D. Ruff and R. Beilharz, 'The Templers in Australia', in J. Jupp (ed.), *The Australian People: An Encyclopedia of the Nation, Its People and Their Origin*, Melbourne, Cambridge University Press, 2001, p. 376.

7   *Willkommen* again

1 Australian Archive, Canberra, A 373, 11570/156 B Pt 2.

2 Australian Archive, Canberra, A 367, C677136.

3 Ibid.

4 J. Tampke and C. Doxford, *Australia Willkommen*, p. 240.

5 Australian Archive, Canberra, A 367, C6/248.

6 G. Kaplan, 'From "Enemy Alien" to Assisted Immigration: Australian Public Opinion of Germans and Germany in the Australian Print Media, 1945 to 1956', in Jurgensen, *German–Australian Cultural Relations since 1945*, p. 89.

7 Voigt, *New Beginnings*, pp. 143–4.

8 Voigt, 'German–Australian Political Relations since 1945', in Jurgensen, *German–Australian Cultural Relations since 1945*, p. 7.

9 G. Kaplan, 'Post War German Immigration', in J. Jupp (ed.), *The Australian People: An Encyclopedia of the Nation, Its People and Their Origins*, Melbourne, Cambridge University Press, 2001, pp. 377–8.

10 R. Barth, Deutsche Einwanderung in Australien seit 1945, MA thesis, Universität Tübingen, 1996, p. 23.

11 Ibid., p. 38; assisted immigration had stopped in 1982.

12 Jupp, 'The Hidden Migrants', p. 64.

13 G. Kaplan, 'Post War German Immigration', p. 378.

14 For some of the better ones, see R. Dengler-McKerchar, *From the Frying Pan into the Fire: Being an Account of Our First Ten Years in the New Country*, Perth, Access Press, 1997; K. A. Cloos, *To Built a Nation's Capital: A Migrant Story*, Canberra, self publication, 2000; Barbara Reif, *The Shepherd's Crook: Memories of a German Migrant in Perth*, Perth, Ginnindera Press, 2002; R. Rack, *The Book of Ruth*, Southern Highland Publishers. See also I. Beinssen, *Fates and Fortunes: Experiences of German Migrants in Australia*, Tübingen, Gunter Narr Verlag, 1987.

15 Voigt, 'German–Australian Political Relations since 1945', p. 8.

16 Voigt, *New Beginnings*, p. 159.

17 Mennicken-Coley, *The Germans in Western Australia*, p. 139.

18 Jupp, 'The Hidden Migrants', pp. 70–1.

19 R. Barth, Deutsche Einwanderung in Australien seit 1945, MA thesis, Universität Tübingen, 1996, p. 85.

20 Cited in ibid., p. 89.

21 Beinssen, *Fates and Fortunes*, p. 11.

22 Mennicken-Coley, *The Germans in Western Australia*, p. 143; K. Petersen, *Zur Situation des Deutschen als Fremdsprache im multikulturellen Australien*, Bern, Peter Lang, 1993, pp. 45–59; Kaplan, 'From "Enemy Alien" to Assisted Immigration', p. 381. On Lodewyckx, see Tampke and Doxford, *Australia Willkommen*, pp. 207–10.

23 Voigt, *New Beginnings*, p. 166; V. Fink, 'Current Aspects in German–Australian Relations', in Jurgensen, *German–Australian Cultural Relations since 1945*, p. 36.

24 G. Stilz, 'German Australian Academic Relations Since 1945', in Jurgensen, *German–Australian Cultural Relations since 1945*, pp. 163–4.

25 P. Truman, 'The German Contribution to Music in Australia since the Second World War', in Jurgensen, *German–Australian Cultural Relations since 1945*, p. 290.

26 Ibid., p. 293.

27 Ibid., pp. 295–300, 302–3.

28 *Australian Dictionary of Biography*, vol. 14, Melbourne, Melbourne University Press, 1996, p. 457.

29 M Brändle, 'German Speaking Painters and Sculptors', in Jurgensen, *German-Australian Cultural Relations since 1945*, pp. 333–4.

30 Jeffries, 'Paul Hirsch Hatvani'.
31 Ibid., p. 93.
32 Tonetto, *Exiled in Language*, p. 158.
33 Ibid., p. 262.

Epilogue

1 S. Castles, 'Democracy and Multicultural Citizenship: Australian Debates and Their Relevance for Western Europe', in R. Bauböck (ed.), *From Aliens to Citizens: Redefining the Status of Immigrants in Europe*, Aldershot UK, Avebury, 1994, p. 7.
2 R. Barth, Deutsche Einwanderung in Australien seit 1945, MA thesis, Universität Tübingen, 1996, pp. 23–5.
3 Ibid., pp. 37–8.
4 R. and M. Munchenberg, *Our Family 125 Years in Australia 1850–1975*, no place, date or publisher.
5 Ibid., p. 32.
6 Mennicken-Coley, *The Germans in Western Australia*, pp. 12–13.
7 L. Kersten and I. Harmstorf, *The Landscape of German-Adelaide: A Walking Tour*, Adelaide, Centre for European Studies, 2001.
8 J. Jennings, 'Leichhardt Expo Event Makes Its Own History', media release, Taroom Council, 8 December 2004, p. 1.
9 Ibid., pp. 2–3.
10 Jupp, *The English in Australia*, p. 182.
11 R. B. Walker, 'German Language Press and People in South Australia 1848–1900', *Journal of the Royal Australian Historical Society*, vol. 58, no. 2, 1972, p. 137.

BIBLIOGRAPHY

Aurousseau, M., *The Letters of F. W. Ludwig Leichhardt*, 3 vols, Cambridge, Cambridge University Press, 1968.

Bade, K. J., *Auswanderer-Wanderarbeiter-Gastarbeiter*, Osterfildern, Scriptae Mercaturae Verlag, 1984.

Bardenhagen, M. E., *Lilydale: A German Legacy*, Launceston, Tasmanian Institute of Technology, 1988.

Bodi, L. and S. Jeffries, *The German Connection*, Melbourne, Department of German, Monash University, 1985.

Brändle, M., 'German Speaking Painters and Sculptors', in Jurgensen (ed.), *German–Australian Cultural Relations since 1945* (see below), pp. 326–41.

Burckhardt, G. and N. Mackay, *History of the German Community in the Clarence River District of NSW*, Grafton, Grafton Family History Centre, 1999.

Castles, S., M. Kalantzis and B. Cope, *Ethnic Conflict and Social Cohesion*, Canberra, Department of Immigration and Ethnic Affairs, 1991.

Clark, C., 'Confessional Policy and the Limits of State Action: Frederick William III and the Prussian Church Union 1817–40', *The History Journal*, vol. 39, no. 4, 1996, pp. 985–1004.

Clark, D., 'Charles von Hügel: Journal of a Visit to Australia and New Zealand', in Harmstorf and Schwerdtfeger, *The German Experience of Australia 1833–1938* (see below), pp. 1–16.

Clark, D. (ed.), *New Holland Journal*, Melbourne, Melbourne University Press, 1994.

Cloos, P. and J. Tampke (eds), *'Greetings from the Land where Milk and Honey Flows': The German Immigration to New South Wales 1838–1858*, Canberra, Southern Highlands Publishers, 1993.

Corkhill, A., 'The German Language Press in Australia and the Mechanics of Survival', in Jurgensen (ed.), *German–Australian Cultural Relations since 1945* (see below), pp. 309–20.

—'German Settlement in Queensland 1838–1939', in J. Jupp (ed.), *The Australian People: An Encyclopedia of the Nation, Its People and Their Origins*, Melbourne, Cambridge University Press, 2001, pp. 369–70.

Darragh, T. A. and R. N. Wuchatsch, *From Hamburg to Hobsons Bay: German Emigration to Port Phillip, 1841–1851*, Melbourne, Wendish Heritage Society, 1999.

Durack, M., *The Rock in the Sand*, London, Constable, 1969.

Harmstorf, I., 'German Settlement in South Australia until 1914', in J. Jupp (ed.), *The Australian People: An Encyclopedia of the Nation, Its People and Their Origins*, Melbourne, Cambridge University Press, 2001, pp. 360–5.

Harmstorf, I. and M. Cigler, *The Germans in Australia*, Melbourne, AE Press, 1985.

Harmstorf, I. and P. Schwerdtfeger, *The German Experience of Australia 1833–1938*, Adelaide, Australian Association of von Humboldt Fellows, 1988.

Jeffries, S., 'Paul Hirsch Hatvani: A German Speaking Expressionist Writer in Victoria', in L. Bodi and S. Jeffries, *The German Connection*, Melbourne, Department of German, Monash University, 1985, pp. 92–4.

Jupp, J., 'The Hidden Migrants: German-Speakers in Australia since 1950', in Jurgensen (ed.), *German–Australian Cultural Relations since 1945* (see below), pp. 63–75.

—*The English in Australia*, Melbourne, Cambridge University Press, 2004.

Jurgensen, M. (ed.), *German–Australian Cultural Relations since 1945*, Berne, Peter Lang, 1995.

Kynaston, E., *A Man on the Edge: A Life of Baron von Müller*, Melbourne, Allen Lane, 1981.

Lodewyckx, A., *Die Deutschen in Australien*, Stuttgart, Ausland und Heimat Verlagsaktiengesellschaft, 1932.

McCredie, A. D., 'German Musical Tradition in South Australia', in Harmstorf and Schwerdtfeger, *The German Experience of Australia 1833–1938* (see above), pp. 54–68.

Mennicken-Coley, M., *The Germans in Western Australia*, Perth, Department of Language Studies, Edith Cowan University, 1993.

Moses, J. A., '"Deutschtumspolitik" in Australia: From Kaiserreich to Third Reich', in Harmstorf and Schwerdtfeger, *The German Experience of Australia 1833–1938* (see above), pp. 120–36.

Sprod, D., 'Leichhardt's Second Expedition 1846–1847: Why Did It Fail?', in H. Lamping and M. Linke (eds), 'Australia: Studies on the History of Discovery and Exploration', *Frankfurter Wirtschafts und Sozialgeographische Schriften*, vol. 65, 1994, pp. 149–68.

Stilz, G., 'German Australian Academic Relations since 1945', in Jurgensen (ed.), *German–Australian Cultural Relations since 1945* (see above), pp. 154–76.

Sumner, R., *A Woman in the Wilderness: The Story of Amalia Dietrich in Australia*, Sydney, University of New South Wales Press, 1993.

Tampke, J., 'Die multikulturelle Gesellschaft der Gegenwart', in R. Bader (ed.), *Australien eine interdisziplinäre Einführung*, Trier, Wissenschaftlicher Verlag, 2002, pp. 115–29.

Tampke, J. (ed.), *'Ruthless Warfare': German Military Planning and Surveillance in the Australian–New Zealand Region before the Great War*, Canberra, Southern Highlands Publishers, 1998.

Tampke, J. and C. Doxford, *Australia Willkommen: A History of the Germans in Australia*, Sydney, University of New South Wales Press, 1990.

Tampke, J. and D. Walker, *From Berlin to the Burdekin: The German Contribution to the Development of Australian Science, Exploration and the Arts*, Sydney, University of New South Wales Press, 1991.

Tipton, F. B., *A History of Germany since 1815*, London, Continuum, 2003.

Tonetto, W., *Exiled in Language: The Poetry of Margaret Diesendorf, Walter Billeter, Rudi Krausmann, und Manfred Jurgensen*, Lewiston NY, Academia Press, 2001.

Truman, P., 'The German Contribution to Music in Australia since the Second World War', in Jurgensen (ed.), *German–Australian Cultural Relations since 1945* (see above), pp. 286–308.

Veit, W., 'In Search of Carl Strehlow: Lutheran Missionary and Australian Anthropologist', in Tampke and Walker, *From Berlin to the Burdekin* (see above), pp. 108–34.

Voigt, J. H., *New Beginnings: The Germans in New South Wales and Queensland*, Stuttgart, Institut für Auslandsbeziehungen, 1983.

—*Australien und Deutschland: 200 Jahre Begegenungen, Beziehungen und Verbindungen*, Hamburg, Institut für Asienkunde, 1988.

—'German–Australian Political Relations since 1945', in Jurgensen (ed.), *German–Australian Cultural Relations since 1945* (see above), pp. 1–17.

Walker, M., *Germany and the Emigration 1816–1885*, Cambridge Mass., Harvard University Press, 1964.

Williams, J. F., *German Anzacs and the First World War*, Sydney, University of New South Wales Press, 2003.

INDEX